# THE
# POODLE

**Front cover:** Ch. Alekai All Together, bred at Mrs. Henry J. Kaiser's kennels. **Back cover:** Ch. Lou Gin's Kiss Me Kate, owned by Terri Meyers and co-owned by Jack and Paulan Phelan.

**Title page photo:** The exquisite Ch. Rimskittle Riot, by Ch. Longleat Alimar Raisin Cane ex Ch. Rimskittle Ruffian, was Best Standard Poodle and Group Second at Westminster Kennel Club in 1984. Owned by Mrs. Margaret Durney, bred by Mr. and Mrs. James Edward Clark, and handled by Tim Brazier.

ISBN 0-86622-033-X

© 1984 by T.F.H. Publications, Inc. Ltd.

Distributed in the UNITED STATES by T.F.H. Publications, Inc., 211 West Sylvania Avenue, Neptune City, NJ 07753; in CANADA by H & L Pet Supplies Inc., 27 Kingston Crescent, Kitchener, Ontario N2B 2T6; Rolf C. Hagen Ltd., 3225 Sartelon Street, Montreal 382 Quebec; in ENGLAND by T.F.H. Publications Limited, 4 Kier Park, Ascot, Berkshire SL5 7DS; in AUSTRALIA AND THE SOUTH PACIFIC by T.F.H. (Australia) Pty. Ltd., Box 149, Brookvale 2100 N.S.W., Australia; in NEW ZEALAND by Ross Haines & Son, Ltd., 18 Monmouth Street, Grey Lynn, Auckland 2 New Zealand; in SINGAPORE AND MALAYSIA by MPH Distributors (S) Pte., Ltd., 601 Sims Drive, # 03/07/21, Singapore 1438; in the PHILIPPINES by Bio-Research, 5 Lippay Street, San Lorenzo Village, Makati Rizal; in SOUTH AFRICA by Multipet Pty. Ltd., 30 Turners Avenue, Durban 4001. Published by T.F.H. Publications Inc., Ltd. the British Crown Colony of Hong Kong.

# THE
# POODLE

## BY ANNA KATHERINE NICHOLAS

## *Dedication*

*To Samantha,*
with love and in appreciation
of the pleasure
she adds to our lives.

# Contents

# About the Author

Since early childhood, Anna Katherine Nicholas has been involved with dogs. Her first pets were a Boston Terrier, an Airedale, and a German Shepherd. Then, in 1925, came the first of the Pekingese—a gift from a friend who raised them. Now her home is shared with a Miniature Poodle and a dozen or so Beagles, including her noted Best in Show dog and National Specialty winner, Champion Rockaplenty's Wild Oats, a Gold Certificate sire (one of the breed's truly great stud dogs), who as a show dog was Top Beagle in the Nation in 1973. She also owns Champion Foyscroft True Blue Lou, Foyscroft Aces Are Wild, and in co-ownership with Marcia Foy, who lives with her, Champion Foyscroft Triple Mitey Migit.

Miss Nicholas is best known throughout the Dog Fancy as a writer and as a judge. Her first magazine article, published in *Dog News* magazine around 1930, was about Pekingese; and this was followed by a widely acclaimed breed column, "Peeking at the Pekingese" which appeared for at least two decades, originally in *Dogdom*, then, following the demise of that publication, in *Popular Dogs*. During the 1940's she was Boxer columnist for *Pure-Bred Dogs/American Kennel Gazette* and for *Boxer Briefs*. More recently many of her articles, geared to interest fanciers of every breed, have appeared in *Popular Dogs, Pure-Bred Dogs/American Kennel Gazette, Show Dogs, Dog Fancy,* and *The World of the Working Dog*. Currently she is a featured regular columnist in *Kennel Review, Dog World,* and *Canine Chronicle*. Her *Dog World* column, "Here, There and Everywhere," was the Dog Writers Association of America winner of the Best Series in a Dog Magazine Award for 1979.

It was during the late 1930's that Miss Nicholas' first book, *The Pekingese*, appeared, published by and written at the request of the Judy Publishing Company. This book completely sold out and is now a collector's item, as is her *The Skye Terrier Book*, which was published by the Skye Terrier Club of America during the early 1960's.

In 1970 Miss Nicholas won the Dog Writers Association of America award for the Best Technical Book of the Year with her *Nicholas Guide to Dog Judging*, published by Howell Book House. In 1979 the revision of this book again won the Dog Writers Association of America

Ch. Camelot's The Fall Guy winning under judge Anna Katherine Nicholas. Bred by Nancy and Marvin Fishler and owned by Nancy, Marvin and Mary Ellen Fishler, Gaithersburg, Maryland.

Best Technical Book Award, the first time ever that a revision has been so honored by this association.

In the early 1970's, Miss Nicholas co-authored, with Joan Brearley, five breed books which were published by T.F.H. Publications, Inc. These were *This is the Bichon Frise, The Wonderful World of Beagles and Beagling* (winner of a Dog Writers Association of America Honorable Mention Award), *The Book of the Pekingese, The Book of the Boxer,* and *This is the Skye Terrier.*

During recent years, Miss Nicholas has been writing books consistently for T.F.H. These include *Successful Dog Show Exhibiting, The Book of the Rottweiler, The Book of the Poodle, The Book of the Labrador Retriever, The Book of the English Springer Spaniel, The Book of the Golden Retriever,* and *The Book of the German Shepherd Dog.* Most recently she has written *The Book of the Shetland Sheepdog,* another breed spectacular, and in the same series with the one you are now reading, *The Chow Chow, The Keeshond, The Cocker Spaniel,* and several additional titles. In the T.F.H. "KW" series, she has done *Rottweilers, Weimaraners,* and *Norwegian Elkhounds.* She has also supplied the American chapters for two English publications, imported by T.F.H., *The Staffordshire Bull Terrier* and *The Jack Russell Terrier.*

Miss Nicholas, in addition to her four Dog Writers Association of America awards, has on two occasions been honored with the *Kennel Review* "Winkie" as Dog Writer of the Year; and in both 1977 and 1982 she was recipient of the Gaines "Fido" award as Journalist of the Year in Dogs.

Her judging career began in 1934 at the First Company Governors' Foot Guard in Hartford, Connecticut, drawing the largest Pekingese entry ever assembled to date at this event. Presently she is approved to judge all Hounds, Terriers, Toys, and Non-Sporting Dogs; all Pointers, English and Gordon Setters, Vizslas, Weimaraners, and Wire-haired Pointing Griffons in Sporting breeds and, in Working Group, Boxers and Doberman Pinschers. In 1970 she became the third woman in history to judge Best in Show at the prestigious Westminster Kennel Club Dog Show, where she has officiated on some sixteen other occasions through the years. In addition to her numerous Westminster assignments, Miss Nicholas has judged at such other outstandingly important events as Santa Barbara, Trenton, Chicago International, the Sportsmans in Canada, the Metropolitan in Canada, and Specialty Shows in several dozen breeds both in the United States and in Canada. She has judged in almost every one of the mainland United States and in four Canadian provinces, and her services are constantly sought in other countries.

Through the years, Miss Nicholas has held important offices in a great many all-breed and Specialty clubs. She still remains an honorary member of several of them.

This is Monsieur, depicted on the Valentines Series Dog Studies probably in the early 1900's.

# Chapter 1

# *Origin and Early Development*

Contrary to popular belief, and despite the fact that he is widely known as "the National Dog of France," the Poodle by origin is not a French breed of dog. In actuality, Germany is the birthplace of the early Poodle, the country where the breed was named, and it was from there, during the revolutionary wars, that the dogs accompanied the troops into France, where they were quickly and enthusiastically adopted.

The name of the breed, "Poodle," is derived from the German word "Pudel," which was how these dogs were known in Germany. It translates as "members of the *Canis familiaris aquaticus*,"—dogs noted for their love of "splashing in water," and known there as "pudelin." Obviously from earliest times Poodles have been water dogs; the Standards particularly are excellent swimmers, have a keen nose, and possess the strength and power to make them outstandingly useful retrievers. The "lion clip" for these dogs was designed with this work in mind, freeing their hindquarters from the burden of superfluous hair and thus enabling them to swim with far less effort.

In France the water-dog instincts of the Poodle were noted with appreciation by duck hunters. There the dogs became known as "Caniche" or "Chien canne," so closely and successfully were they associated with this sport.

Equalling the breed's popularity in Germany and in France was that bestowed upon it in Russia. Each of these three countries had their own standard of perfection drawn up for the breed; all three versions appear in my big *The Book of the Poodle* also published by T.F.H. and obtainable wherever the one you are reading was purchased. It is interesting to note the differences between these early Poodle standards

Early German Poodles on a post card—from back in the days when this really *was* a "penny" (1¢ postage) post card!

and the part they have played in the dog we know today. Actually, Poodles have changed little over the generations, still being basically the same impressive dogs as then except for the refinements of the earlier type and subsequent development.

Although the Poodle was originally most widely used as a sporting dog, there was also appreciation of the cleverness, intelligence, and superiority of the breed's personality, and the smaller ones became great favorites with the ladies as pets. Poodles seem to possess an inborn ability to entertain, and many gained fame owing to their natural tendency to walk on their hind legs (or "dance" as it was accepted to be) and their quick aptitude for learning to work together in almost incredibly outstanding performances as entertainers. In those days they were part of almost every circus, as is still the case, and many a Poodle has earned acclaim for the marvelous feats he or she has learned to perfection. Hundreds of troupes of performing Poodles through the years have provided amusement and pleasure to children of all ages!

While the large Poodles were proving their worth as sportsmen's companions in the field, the smaller varieties also were useful in another form of "retrieving"—working as "truffle dogs." This con-

Corded Poodles from Germany early in this century.

sisted of sniffing out and digging up the edible fungus known as a "truffle"—considered a rare delicacy by many people. Only small light-footed dogs with a keen sense of smell were suitable for the work of locating and removing the truffle without breaking it, an art in which the small Poodle excelled since it was perfectly equipped for it with its sharp nose and small, light feet. The smaller Poodle became famous for this aptitude since the truffle industry was highly lucrative. There are those who claim that a terrier outcross was introduced in these "Truffle Poodles," which may or may not have been true. The author's thinking on this is that only a dog so light-footed and dainty of touch as a tiny Poodle could perform this delicate task efficiently and that the terrier paw would be too rough.

In appearance, the "Truffle Poodles" are said to have been mostly black and white in coloring, sometimes black heads and tails on white bodies or white spotted with black patches. Some of the "Truffle Poodles" shown in England, where they at one time had their own classification, have been described as having heavy, hard-textured coats and that many were short-backed with lovely long, lean heads.

Almost certainly these were the ancestors of the original Toy Poodle.

15

The exquisite bitch Halloween of Montfleuri, by Eng. Ch. Union Jack of Montfleuri ex Eng. Ch. Hannaka of Montfleuri, at fourteen months of age. Halloween at this time was already winner of ten first prizes, seven times Best Puppy, two Challenge Certificates, four Reserve Challenge Certificates, and Senior Warrant from the only ten shows at which she had been exhibited. She is one of the many magnificent Montfleuri black Miniatures of Mrs. N. Howard Price, Cowden, Kent, England.

# Chapter 2

# *Poodles in Great Britain*

So versatile and attractive a dog as the Poodle was bound to receive a warm reception in Great Britain. As far back as the 1860's the breed was creating interest, with the foundation of the Poodle Club of England taking place in 1886, followed quickly by the preparation and adoption of Great Britain's first standard for the breed.

From 1900 until World War I, the British Poodle made steady progress. In the earliest days, the corded coat style seemed to take precedence over the curly coats, and Standard Poodles outnumbered the Miniatures, while the Toys at that time were a separate breed entirely, when seen at all. Gradually the corded coats waned in popularity with the curlies increasing in favor, largely, I am sure, because of the difficulty of properly caring for the cords and keeping them tidy, clean-smelling and well groomed.

In the minds of most people in the beginning, all Poodles were thought of as being Standards, but when the Miniatures started to appear (developed from breeding down in size from small Standards) their appeal was instant. As for the Toys, it was well into the 1900's before they actually joined the Poodle family. More about this in a later chapter.

Outstanding early English Poodle breeders made notable contributions to breed progress in both England and, through their exports, in the United States. One of the earliest and most influential was Miss Brunker of the Whippendells, who made her presence felt in both Miniatures and Standards starting as long ago as 1895 when she brought out the first blue Miniature shown in England, Pierette Jackson. In 1929 she became the breeder of the historic Standard dog Whippendell Poli, who came to the United States to blaze a trail of glory for the breed.

The Barbet Poodles were owned by Mrs. Crimmins and she had some very excellent ones. Mrs. Jack Taylor was an important English breeder who sent some notable Miniatures to the United States, and Mrs. Tyndall's Vendas Kennels made considerable contribution to Miniature quality.

A noteworthy Miniature, born in 1927, was Champion Spriggan Bell, a leading winner and top producer. This dog was owned by Mrs. Arthur Willets, who also had a very pretty silver Miniature, Champion The Ghost.

As this book is a small one by comparison with our *The Book of the Poodle,* we shall not attempt to give complete coverage in it of dogs and people. Rather we shall select a kennel or two in each case to use as an example and to acquaint our readers with some of the many outstanding Poodles and people in various parts of the world. We shall give highlights from each area.

To select a highly influential British breeder of Miniatures and one of Standards, the first people who come to mind are Mrs. G.E.L. Boyd of the Piperscrofts for the Miniatures and Miss Jane Lane of the Nunsoes for Standards.

With her Piperscroft Poodles, Mrs. Boyd specialized in black Miniatures, but she also had a fondness for and activity in white and silver Miniatures and, to a lesser degree, in Standards. This lady was a superb breeder and thoroughly knowledgeable fancier, as any student of the Poodle breed can affirm.

Mrs. Boyd's foundation stock in Miniatures included two whites imported to England from Germany, purchased from Mrs. Crimmins when Barbet Poodles were disbanded. These dogs are credited with having had a strongly beneficial influence on improved heads and pigmentation on small white Poodles in Great Britain. She also availed herself promptly of the opportunity to bring to Piperscroft many of the Chieveley Miniatures when it became possible to do so, adding these excellent Miniatures to her own stock at Piperscroft, where they helped to create famous and influential dogs around the Poodle world. It was one of the Chieveley Miniatures, eight years old at the time, Chieveley Chopstick, who became the first Miniature to gain championship in the United States in 1933. His grandson, Champion Ramoneur of Catawba, became the first Miniature to win the West-

Ch. Vulcan Champagne Damassin and daughter Vulcan Champagne Hosanna. Damassin, by Vulcan Champagne Admirer ex Ch. Vulcan Champagne Dimity, was bred by Miss S. Walne and owned by Miss A.C. Coppage. She was the first Standard Miss Coppage owned and handled to her title, was her personal pet, and "a perfect lady," to quote her owner. Her litter sister, Vulcan Champagne Silk, also became a champion and was a foundation bitch for the line of Beguinette whites. Damassin is the great-great-grandmother of the three Swedish imports now owned by Miss Coppage. Vulcan Poodles, Taunton, Somerset, England.

minster Kennel Club Non-Sporting Group in the United States nine years later, to be succeeded in the following year by another famed descendant, Champion Pitter Patter of Piperscroft, who became the first Miniature to win Best in Show at Westminster.

Mrs. Boyd was the first Poodle breeder in Great Britain to train dogs for police work and the first to appear with Poodles in the obedience ring. She also was the first English judge to officiate at a Poodle Specialty in the United States, where she judged both Interstate and the Poodle Club of America, and where her services were greatly in demand.

It was Mrs. Boyd who showed the first son of Tri-International Champion Nunsoe Duc de la Terrace of Blakeen to appear in the British show rings. This dog was Knight of Piperscroft, by Duc ex Samite of Piperscroft (litter-sister to Champion Nunsoe Nikola's Christopher Robin). He triumphed in some good competition before being sold to the United States.

In the Standard world, Miss Jane Lane was known and admired far and wide as the owner of the Nunsoes, and she was without a doubt England's foremost Standard breeder of her day. Her foundation bitch was one from Whippendell breeding, Nunsoe Aunt Chloe, who was by Whippendell Drapeau although actually bred by Mrs. Lovett. Another of her famous Standards was the black Champion Nunsoe Lady Mary.

Miss Lane, appreciating the quality dogs being produced at Madame Reichanbach's renowned Labory Kennels in Switzerland, acquired some of them to blend into her own breeding program. Among those coming to her in 1932 was that immortal dog Duc, (Champion Nunsoe Duc de la Terrace of Blakeen) of whom you will read further in the United States section of this book. Duc remained at Nunsoe only for a short while; but four splendid litters by him remained behind when he left England, in addition to the one already mentioned at Mrs. Boyd's.

As the 1900's progressed, many other kennels became famous in England; these kennels were owned by dedicated breeders whose contributions still are being felt. In the Miniature world, Alida Monroe of the Firebrave Kennels stands among the foremost. Then the Merrymorns carved a niche in the history of the Miniature and Toy Poodles. Montmartre produced the background for many great and outstanding Miniatures, and there also was Braevel, whence has come some of the finest.

To bring you an idea of what is taking place currently in Great Britain's Poodle world, we have selected two of the finest, Montfleuri for

The lovely Eng. Ch. Springett Cambrai's Camille, stunning white bitch, born in 1973, is the offspring of two Canadian imports, by Ch. Bibelot's Polar de la Fontaine of Springett ex Springett Park Quite The Lady of Bibelot. Bred by Mrs. M. Willis. Owned by Miss A.C. Coppage, Vulcan Poodles, Taunton, Somerset, England.

The famous white bitch Ch. Vulcan Champagne Damassin owned by Miss A.C. Coppage, Vulcan Champagne Kennels, England.

Miniatures and Vulcan for the Standards, both of whom we feel are, and have been from the beginning, producing dogs of tremendous quality who have influenced Poodles to be found around the world. Many are the countries where the descendants of dogs from these kennels are being pointed to with pride!

The foundation of Montfleuri Poodles was well thought out and carefully planned by Philippe Howard Price when he first became involved with the breed back in the 1940's. The kennel was based on England's foremost bloodlines, and its owner used them well. When Nadia and Philippe Howard Price were married, in 1962, Montfleuri became a joint project, the interest and management of the kennel shared by both parties. Gradually Philippe's antiques business became increasingly time-consuming, leaving more and more of the kennel responsibility to be assumed by his wife. But she was, and is, well equal to it, so things ran on smoothly.

Philippe Howard Price passed away of a heart attack quite suddenly and at only 53 years of age—a tremendous shock and a great loss to his friends and to the Poodle world.

Fortunately, however, Nadia Howard Price has steadily maintained her love of and interest in the Poodles. Her enthusiasm is as warm today as when she first began, and she runs the kennel with a partner, Rosemary Lee. She is also involved in Arabian horses, at Corden, in Kent. Her ambition so far as the Poodles are concerned is to maintain the values and high standards held over these past four decades. She is succeeding!

English Champion Milord of Mannerhead, by English Champion The Laird of Mannerhead ex Miladi of Mannerhead, was Montfleuri's first champion, followed very swiftly by a whole series of superb dogs who gained their titles. Particularly memorable among the early ones were English Champion Figaro of Montfleuri, English Champion Lady Gay of Montfleuri, and English Champion Valentina of Montfleuri.

It was in 1954 that the tiny black Tresor De Madjise was imported to Montfleuri from France. She became a champion and produced English Champion Toomai of Montfleuri, by Harwell of Mannerhead.

The widely admired Best in Show Champion Braebeck Toni of Montfleuri (winner of twelve Challenge Certificates) and his almost equally famous sisters, Champion Braebeck Jonella of Montfleuri (with nine Challenge Certificates) and Champion Trilla of Montfleuri (with eleven Challenge Certificates), soon followed—these by Firebrave Spiro of Braebeck from a Piperscroft bitch.

Vulcan Champagne Soloist is the present show girl at this famous kennel. Miss A.C. Coppage, owner, Taunton, Somerset, England.

**Opposite page:** Nadia Howard Price with Eng. Ch. Mickey Finn of Montfleuri at ten years of age winning the Group at Windsor in 1978.

As the years have passed, Montfleuri has continued to flourish. Although all of the leading winners from there are too numerous to list in this chapter, one must speak of the brothers Champion Moenfarm Marcelle of Montfleuri and Champion Moenfarm Mascot of Mont- fleuri and of Champion Patrick Casey of Montfleuri who, when bred to the Best in Show winner of nineteen Challenge Certificates, Cham- pion Montfleuri Sarah of Lonsnor, sired Champion Tarka of Mont- fleuri, a Best in Show winner with 21 Challenge Certificates.

Tarka, in turn, produced probably the most distinguished of all the Montfleuris, Champion Mickey Finn, with the enviable total of 29 Challenge Certificates to his credit, 29 times Best of Breed, runner-up to Dog Of The Year, all-breeds, a few years back (beaten by a mere two points!), and winner of many Specialty and all-breed Bests in Show. Champion Mickey Finn of Montfleuri came out of retirement at nine and a half years of age during the late 1970's to win the Group at Windsor—indeed a noteworthy accomplishment!

It is interesting to contemplate the stature of these three generations of Poodles and what they have meant to the Miniature Poodle breed: Sarah with her nineteen Challenge Certificates as the dam of Tarka with his 21 Challenge Certificates, he in turn the sire of Mickey Finn with his 29 Challenge Certificates and 29 Bests of Breed. Mrs. Howard Price points out that Mickey Finn is the only Miniature Poo- dle dog never defeated by the bitch, always going Best of Breed each time he won the dog Challenge Certificates. These three Poodles cer- tainly represent a dynasty of quality and success in the Poodle world!

The line is continuing through Mickey Finn whose most prominent offspring include Union Jack of Montfleuri who is in turn the sire of a smashing young black bitch, Halloween of Montfleuri. The latter, even as a puppy, already has created no small furor, what with the winning of ten first prizes, seven Best Puppy Awards, and two Challenge Certificates, all prior to January 1984, at less than fourteen months of age. She is from Hannaka of Montfleuri. In speaking of Halloween, Nadia Howard Price says, "We rate her on a par with her grandsire, the illustrious Champion Mickey Finn of Montfleuri," which is strong and would seem to be well-deserved praise.

Famed throughout the Standard Poodle world, Vulcan Poodles, or Vulcan-Champagne as they are sometimes known, are owned by Miss A.C. Coppage at Taunton, Somerset, England. These dogs are known far and wide, owned and admired in Europe, North America, and Australia as well as in Great Britain.

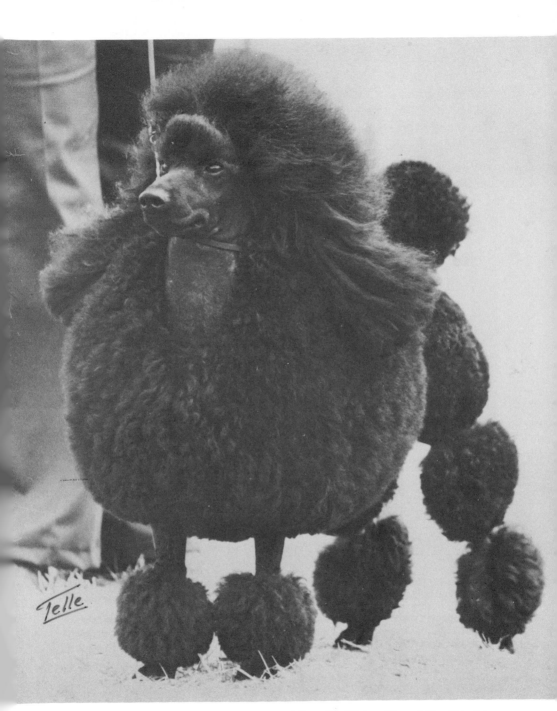

Eng. Ch. Union Jack of Montfleuri, son of Eng. Ch. Mickey Finn of Montfleuri ex Angela of Montfleuri, is another of the superb black Miniatures owned by Mrs. N. Howard Price, Cowden, Kent, England.

The three Swedish imports at Vulcan Kennels in 1983. *Left to right:* Chicos Quick Silver at Vulcan, silver dog; Chicos Qwinna Blue Sign at Vulcan, blue bitch; and Chicos Quality White Star, white dog. Owned by Miss A.C. Coppage, Taunton, Somerset, England.

**Opposite page:** Ch. Vulcan Psyche of Gayshaws from a painting. Miss A.C. Coppage, owner, Taunton, Somerset, England.

Eng. Ch. Cocomar Commander, by Pepsidee Percy Vere ex Aesthete Kissin Secret. Bred, owned, and shown by Mrs. Margaret Gee, Cocomar Toy Poodles.

An astute and talented fancier, Miss Coppage admired the Wycliffe dogs belonging to Mrs. Jean Lyle in Canada; thus she imported a dog from there who has proven a tremendous asset to her kennel. This is Champion Wycliffe Ovation for Vulcan, son of the handsome Champion Wycliffe Fitzherbert, a black male who became a Best in Show winner for Miss Coppage and who is now a famed sire. He has champion progeny to his credit in the United Kingdom, Australia, Finland, Sweden, and Trinidad.

The blue bitch, Champion Vulcan Champagne Ovature, is a daughter of Ovation from Vulcan Wish Upon a Star. Bred by Miss Coppage, she is owned by Mr. and Mrs. Creed and she has been a very excellent producer. Her dam, Wish Upon A Star, is a truly special bitch. Sired by Playhouse the Demon King ex Vulcan Psychedelic, she is herself a Best in Show winner, but her greatest contribution and claim to fame has been as a producer. She carries, it was discovered, a silver gene; and bred to Champion Vulcan April Fancy, she became dam of the silver bitch Champion Vulcan Champagne Starturn and the silver male French and International Champion Vulcan Passing Fancy. In her last litter, sired by Ovation, she produced, along with the aforementioned Ovature, Australian Champion Vulcan Champagne Ovalord, whose influence in that country has been considerable.

In 1982, Miss Coppage imported three puppies from Sweden, grandchildren of Wish Upon A Star. There is a silver male whom she hopes will carry on the good work done by his grandam. He is Chicos Quicksilver at Vulcan, by Vulcan Champagne Star Sign ex Chicos Jolene Mystic, and he was bred by U.L. Lindensparr in Sweden.

Wish Upon A Star is now retired, enjoying life as one of Miss Coppage's house pets—a luxury she has certainly well earned through the quality of progeny she has presented to her breed.

There is in England a kennel featuring Toy Poodles of which we have heard some very nice things. This is Cocomar, owned by Margaret Gee, at Newark, Nottinghamshire.

This very enthusiastic breeder-owner-handler has just made her first champion, a handsome little black dog named English Champion Cocomar Commander, by Pepsidee Percy-Vere ex Aesthete Kissing Secret. "Willie" has four Challenge Certificates, four Reserve Certificates, and three Bests of Breed on the occasions of winning his Challenge Certificates. He is also a Best in Show winner.

Mrs. Gee has been breeding for sixteen years now, concentrating on black and brown Toys. Presently two 9″-Toys are being campaigned. They are a brown bitch, Cocomar Carrimin, sired by Vernlil Home Brew for Cocomar ex Cocomar Caramel; and Cocomar I'm A Cracker, by the same sire, Cracker, a black.

Spanish Champion Bodebi Bobolink with Cocomar is now in Spain, living with Grete Fisher. This little dog was Reserve Challenge Certificate at Crufts in 1983. There also is Cocomar Cadet, who as a puppy went to Spain in June 1983; Cadet has won three Best Puppy awards and one Best Junior award at all-breed championship shows.

Cocomar Chip-Monk is a lovely black bitch by Bobolink who has been doing well for Mrs. Gee with a Challenge Certificate and numerous Junior Warrants to her credit as we write.

Eng. and Am. Ch. Foreman of Tranchant with handler F.C. Dickey and judge Anna Katherine Nicholas. A lovely Best in Show black Miniature of the 1970's.

# Chapter 3

# *History and Development in the United States*

One Poodle, the first to be registered in the United States, appeared in the Stud Book in 1890. Two joined this one the following year, and in 1893 the new Poodle registrations amounted to twenty.

By 1915 Poodle registrations jumped to 245, but then by the close of World War I in 1918 the number had dropped back to 42 Poodles with two Toy Poodles, then a separate breed. Miniature and Standards were at this time both grouped under the heading "Poodles."

The earliest consistent Poodle exhibitors in the United States of whom we are aware were two ladies from Great Neck, Long Island, namely Miss Lucille Alger and Miss Louise Grace. Theirs was the Red Brook Kennel, and they were dominant in Poodle activities in America prior to World War I. These ladies were actually the first of the big-time Poodle exhibitors, and they provided a sampling of what was to follow. They often put ten or more of their dogs into competition (as did the leading kennels of the 1930's) at a single event, grooming and handling them personally and, of course, habitually dominating the winners circle when the awards were made. It was these ladies who inaugurated the custom of brushing out the Poodle coat as we do it today; this was at a time when most other exhibitors were dampening them down to bring in a tighter curl. Importations belonging to this kennel were Champion Orchard Sunstorm and Champion Windward Sauteur. The homebreds included Champion Red Brook Lightfoot who built up an imposing record. It is regrettable that this kennel

Some very celebrated Poodles competed for Best of Breed at the 1955 Poodle Club of America Specialty. *Left to right,* the Standard, Ch. Alfonco v.d. Goldenen Kette owned by Clairedale and Pennyworth Kennels and handled by Robert S. Forsyth. The Miniature, Ch. Fircot L'Ballerine of Maryland handled for Mr. and Mrs. Saunders L. Meade's Seafren Kennels by Ruth Burnette Sayres, and the Toy, Ch. Wilbur White Swan, handled by Anne Hone Rogers Clark for Bertha Smith. These three Best in Show winners made Poodle history with their spectacular show ring successes.

became inactive during the war, as was evidently the case since we have found or read little about any activity on their part after that period.

Interestingly, two outstanding Toy Poodle breeders had their roots in the 'teens, both kennels located in the Philadelphia area. They were owned by Mr. and Mrs. Hartmann and Mrs. Bertha Peaster respectively. The Hartmanns had the first American Toy Poodle champion.

A little girl who saw her first Poodle in 1912, and who grew up to become Mrs. Leonard W. Bonney, lost her heart to the breed way back then. A love for Poodles and for dog shows, which continued well past the first half of this century and which grew to include Chow Chows and Dalmatians along with the Poodles, was the result—this was, I am sure, hardly foreseen when this youngster purchased a Poodle puppy as a gift for her mother!

One is inclined to think of the 1920's in the Poodle world as having been the calm preceding the storm, which started to develop toward their close. Only a few fanciers were raising Poodles at that time, registrations ranging around two dozen annually with perhaps a dozen or so Toy Poodles each year. Show entries, naturally, followed a similar course. The Hartmanns were consistent with their Toys, as was Bertha Peaster. And a lady in Massachusetts, Mrs. Reuben Slote, had a *black* Toy Poodle which was probably the first Toy other than white to be seen in the United States.

As the 1920's drew to a close, things started shaping up in the Poodle world, especially in the New York area where Alice Lang Rogers (Mrs. Byron Rogers) added Poodles to her Misty Isles Kennels at Bedford Hills, New York, already famous for Cairn Terriers. Very quickly

A class of Standard Poodles at the Ladies Kennel Ass'n. Dog Show in 1946.

Alice Rogers became a dominant figure in the early Poodle world, earning the respect of the fancy as a "Poodle person" who helped start numerous others on their way. Alice Rogers is often thought of as having been the mother of Anne Rogers Clark, which is incorrect. Anne's mother was Olga Hone Rogers—Mrs. William Rogers—and she was also a very successful pioneer Poodle breeder; and to make it an even closer coincidence, both ladies lived in the same general area. Alice Rogers had Misty Isles Kennels. Olga Rogers had Surrey, the kennel prefix her daughter still uses in combination with her husband's kennel name, Rimskittle.

Mrs. Whitehouse Walker, together with her father Henry Whitehouse, joined the Poodle Fancy in the late 1920's, laying the foundation for her Carillon Poodles. She was to become one of the pioneers in obedience in the United States, as well as a famed and successful Poodle breeder. These two fanciers were very much involved in the foundation of the Poodle Club of America. Also, it was Mrs. Walker who imported the aforementioned (English chapter) English Standard, Whippendell Poli of Carillon, the first Poodle to win a Non-Sporting Group at Westminster.

With the dawning of the 1930's, Poodle interest in the United States was truly off and running. Obviously a Specialty Club was needed, and the Poodle Club of America was founded in 1931 with a charter membership of ten people. American Kennel Club membership was sought in July of that year, and granted. The first slate of officers consisted of Mr. Whitehouse as President, Mrs. Delancey K. Jay as Vice-President, and Mrs. Walker as Secretary-Treasurer; and the Board consisted of the officers plus Mrs. Leo Brady, H.G. Erwin, Mrs. William Jacobs, Loring Marshall, and Byron Rogers. Mr. Marshall was the Poodle Club of America's first delegate to the American Kennel Club.

The very first problem to confront the Poodle Club of America was the drawing up of a standard for the breed to apply in the United States, and there was evidently considerable divided opinion and discussion before the matter was settled. This was caused by the fact that while actually, until that time, the dogs in America had inclined to be more of the German type than the Anglo-French, many of the fanciers felt, as was the case in England, that the Poodle they preferred was the type being raised in England where the Curly Poodle Club had elected to adopt the French standard. Finally it was settled that the Poodle Club of America would seek permission of the Curly Poo-

Ch. Challenge of Pixiecroft, owned by Mark Crawford and Ted Doucette, won Best in Show from Louis Murr at Onandaga K.A. in 1961. Anne Rogers Clark, handler.

dle Club of England to adopt their standard to apply to the breed in America; this was granted. The standard was submitted to the American Kennel Club and was formally approved and adopted.

The immediate result of this standard was a move to bring from England Poodles which would comply with its requirements; and so the rush was underway, with Poodles crossing the Atlantic on a very steady basis. It must be said in praise of American breeders that they used these importations well and that from them were bred and raised in the United States some of the most correct and excellent, typey, elegant, entirely beautiful Poodles the breed has ever seen.

The standard was approved in 1932, which was the same year the Poodle Club of America held its first Specialty show, which took place in conjunction with the North Westchester Kennel Club All Breed Dog Show at Mt. Kisco, New York, and judged by the Brooklyn all-'rounder, Leon J. Iriberry. The event drew an entry of 23 Poodles (no Toys; Miniatures and Standards under one classification). Champion Whippendell Poli of Carillon added another first to his accomplishments by taking this Best of Breed for Mrs. Walker, while five-point majors were awarded to the imported Nymphaea Jason in dogs and Blakeen Roulette of Misty Isles in bitches.

The latter was one of the first two champions owned by Mr. and Mrs. Sherman R. Hoyt whose Blakeen Kennels were established with the purchase of this bitch and a dog, Blakeen Paul of Misty Isles, by Mrs. Hoyt as a birthday gift for her husband. They were born in 1931, sired by the imported Nymphaea Pice from the also-imported bitch Anita v. Lutterspring, and bred by Alice Lang Rogers, from whom Mrs. Hoyt made the purchase. The importance of this event is almost awe-inspiring when one realizes that this was not only the Hoyts' first champion but also the first Poodle champion bred by Mrs. Rogers and when one stops to consider the aggregate number of champions the Hoyts and Mrs. Rogers owned and/or bred over the following years.

Once the matters of organization and the breed standard had been settled, the Poodle Club of America next turned its attention to the plight of the Miniature Poodle which was in great need of assistance at this time owing to the single classification. No matter how good a Miniature might have been in those days, it was extremely difficult for the small Poodle to hold his own in competition against the better known Standard size, and Miniature fanciers were finding it an uphill climb to gain a title on even the best of their dogs. The Poodle Club of America went to bat on their behalf and succeeded in bringing about

At Ox Ridge in 1948, Mrs. Sherman R. Hoyt wins the Non-Sporting Group with Ch. Blakeen Osprey, one of the leading white Standards of the day.

separate classifications for Miniatures and Standards through the classes, so that each variety had its own Winners Dog and Winners Bitch and the opportunity of earning championship points. A Best of Variety in each size was selected; but then a Best of Breed was judged, which enabled only one Poodle, the winner of that final competition, to appear in the Non-Sporting Group. Eventually the present system of judging each variety as a separate breed, and both (Miniature and Standard) competing in the Group, was adopted. There is talk of reverting to the former way again, which this writer sincerely hopes will not come to pass.

Now the Miniatures started to add the titles to their names! The first Miniature champion to finish in the United States was the imported dog mentioned in our British chapter, Champion Chieveley Chop-

The famed Toy Poodle, Ch. Blakeen Ding Ding, owned by Mrs. Marguerite S. Tyson winning Best in Show, with Maxine Beam, handler and Charles A. Swartz, judge, at Jacksonville, Florida, January 1956.

stick, who had been sold to Charles Price of Boston, Massachusetts. The second Mini to finish was Champion King Johnny and the third, Whippendell Picot, was the latter's half-brother.

1933 was the year, already mentioned, when Champion Whippendell Poli became the first Poodle to win the Westminster Non-Sporting Group. Blakeen Poodles made their Westminster debut that year, too, taking Winners Dog and Winners Bitch with Paul and Roulette respectively. And Mr. and Mrs. Justin W. Griess, whose Salmagundi Poodles were to become so successful and prominent, made their first champion, a brown Standard bitch named Victoria, who subsequently became the dam of their first homebred to finish.

The magnificent white Standard Poodle Ch. Ensarr Cygne with his breeder-owner, Mrs. W. French Githens, winning one of many Non-Sporting Groups this very handsome dog amassed during his show career, this time at Rockland County in 1953, the judge William L. Kendrick.

1933 was also the year when Mrs. T. Whitney Blake purchased a very special gift for her daughter and son-in-law, Mr. and Mrs. Sherman R. Hoyt, in the form of what the Hoyts had told her was the finest Poodle they had ever seen: Tri-International Champion Nunsoe Duc de la Terrace of Blakeen.

Duc made his first Westminster appearance at Madison Square Garden in 1934, going from the classes to first in the Non-Sporting Group, only the second Poodle ever to have done so. He gained some other nice honors, too, prior to his return the following year; but when he entered the Garden in 1935, he did not leave there until he had won the breed, the Group, *and Best in Show,* making himself the first Poodle to attain such heights at this show and Hayes Hoyt the first woman ever to have handled a Westminster Best in Show winner to the honor! Highlights of Poodle history—how exciting to recall! Duc won the Group again in 1936 for the third time.

The first American-bred Miniature championship was completed in 1934, a black daughter of Champion Chieveley Chopstick from a daughter of Champion King Johnny and a Standard bitch. Chieveley Chopstick's influence was to be felt further along, too, as we will note.

Mrs. Milton Erlanger, a lady who was to achieve a position of enormous prominence and influence in the breed, appeared on the Poodle scene in the mid-1930's. Her first homebred champion, Cadeau de Noel, was by Stillington Christmas of Carillon from Nunsoe the Mite, followed shortly thereafter by the first two bearing her own kennel prefix, Champion Pillicoc Toisin D'Or and Champion Pillicoc Vedette. Champion Cadeau de Noel further distinguished herself by becoming the dam of the noted Champion Pillicoc Rumpelstiltskin, one of the most famed and admired dogs in Poodle history, who was handled, as were Mrs. Erlanger's other Poodles, by Henry Stoecker, now so widely admired and knowledgeable an all-breed judge.

Other mid-1930's happenings included the completion of the championship of Champion Edelweiss du Labory of Salmagundi, Duc's half-brother, as an addition to the growing champion roster at Salmagundi Kennels; the first homebred for the Hoyts, Champion Blakeen Mary Mont, a black bitch; and the completed titles of Champion Blakeen Cyrano and Champion Blakeen Durante, two glorious brown dogs. The former was sold to Miss Mary McCreery for her Lowmont Kennels, becoming the first Poodle exportation from the United States to England.

The first silver Standard to finish, Champion Griseley Labory of Piperscroft of Blakeen, did so in 1935, as did two Miniatures of this color.

By 1936 Poodle enthusiasm had made it to the West Coast, where the interest, which was to contribute so greatly to Poodle achievement in the United States, of Ernest E. Ferguson had started to stir. Ernie purchased Champion Knight of Piperscroft of Blakeen for his Estid Kennels, the first at a Poodle headquarters which has accommodated some of the most fabulous Miniatures and Standards of all time.

The first California-bred Poodle champion was a black bitch, Champion Roulette of Fair Acres. The first Miniature champion bred there was also the first of the homebred Poodle champions owned by Lydia Hopkins of Sherwood Hall Kennels.

The 1930's closed in pretty much the same manner as the decade had opened, with Poodles flourishing. But what an enormous amount of progress had been made! Closing out the decade were two club events of deep importance to the breed: the recognition of a second Specialty club, the Interstate Poodle Club, and the holding of its first Specialty Show; and the Poodle Club of America's first independent Specialty (held on its own as a separate event, not in conjunction with any all-breed show).

Two early Standard Poodle "greats," Ch. Blakeen Cyrano and Ch. Blakeen Durante, bred by the Blakeen Kennels, Mr. and Mrs. Sherman R. Hoyt, then at Katonah, New York. From a painting by Robert Borton dated 1935.

Ch. Encore Jester, black Toy male owned by Mrs. Jane Fitts, was widely admired during the 1950's.

Ch. Prankster Darius, Standard Poodle, winning Best in Show at the Great Lakes Poodle Club of Chicago Specialty, April 1959. William J. Trainor handling for Prankster Kennels. Mrs. Jesse Mason judge.

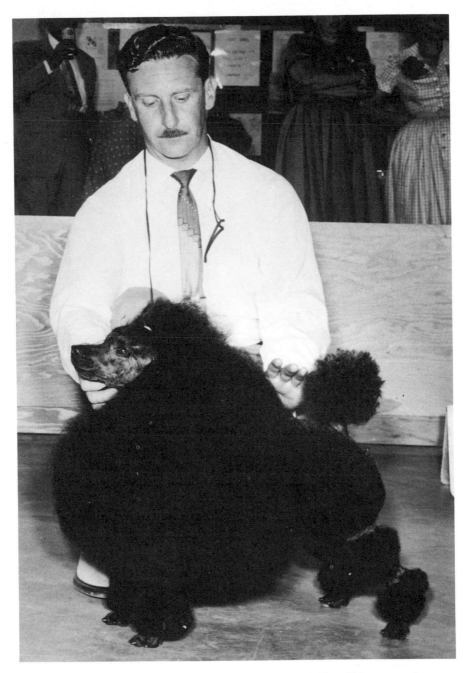

Ch. Highland Sand George, owned by Mr. James Farrell, Tiro, Ohio, was an important winner of the 1950's and early 1960's. Tom Crowe handling him to Best of Variety, Greater Cincinnati Poodle Club Specialty.

Ch. Puttencove Promise taking Best in Show at Springfield, Massachussetts November 1957, under judge Alva Rosenberg. Owned by Puttencove Kennels, Mr. and Mrs. George Putnam. Handled by Robert Gorman.

Interstate had been formed as the result of the feeling that, considering the rate of growth of Poodle popularity, the breed's best interests would be more efficiently served by the addition of a second Specialty club devoted to it. The people behind this project were Mr. and Mrs. Hoyt; Mr. and Mrs. George Putnam, who had become exceedingly active breeders and exhibitors through their Puttencove Kennels (Mrs. Putnam is about the only Poodle breeder from this era who is still exhibiting Poodles today, although on a limited scale); Mrs. Irene Stowell Morse of the Diablotin Miniatures, an excellent breeder whose black Miniatures were behind many important winners; Mr. and Mrs. W. French Githens, breeder-owners of some very outstanding Standards and owners of the successful Miniature Champion Ensarr Salute; and Mr. and Mrs. Hugh Chisholm whose Strathglass

Kennels were known for lovely Miniatures. These, and several other respected breeders, were the backbone of Interstate; and through their combined efforts, this club had enormous impact. There were at this time no Poodle Club of America affiliated clubs. Interstate asked permission to become an A.K.C. member club as was P.C.A. The request obviously had merit as the application was approved, making Poodles the first breed to have two Specialty clubs sharing equal responsibility for the future of their breed.

Interstate's first Specialty was held in May 1938 for American-breds only, judged by the renowned English breeder Mrs. Boyd. Best Standard and Best of Breed was won by Blakeen Kennels with the white bitch Champion Blakeen Jung Frau. Miniatures and Best of Opposite Sex went to the Miniature dog Champion Cheri of Misty Isles who had come through from the classes.

Mrs. Marguerite S. Tyson, the very lovely lady who owned the Ty-Del Poodles, with her great white Miniature Ch. Adastra Magic Fame.

A group of the
Salmagundi Poodles
owned by Mr. and
Mrs. Justin W.
Greiss. Famous win-
ners of the
mid-1900's.

At the Poodle Club of America first independent Specialty, Champion Pillicoc Rumpelstiltskin won Standards and Best in Show, while Champion Cheri of Misty Isles, now shown as a Special, led Miniatures.

Also in 1938, Champion Blakeen Jung Frau won the Non-Sporting Group at Morris and Essex. Champion Pillicoc Rumpelstiltskin did likewise at Westminster.

Miniatures really had hit their stride by 1939, with some fabulous new dogs appearing from Mrs. P.H.B. Frelinghuysen's kennels, Mrs. Meade's Seafren Kennels (formerly mainly interested in Standards), and Mrs. James M. Austin's Catawba Kennels (where Champion Vendas The Black Imp of Catawba arrived, among others); Pillicoc Kennels had become Miniature-conscious, as had Miriam Hall at Cartlane.

The '40's started out with a "first" when Mrs. Austin's Toy Poodle, Karetina of Muriclar, who had been bred by Muriel Clark in California, became the first Toy Poodle to win a Group in the United States, doing so at Westminster—surely a very spectacular place in which to have accomplished it!

This was the year in which Champion Blakeen Jung Frau won Best in Show at Morris and Essex, the largest dog show in the United States ever won by a Poodle. Some years later a Miniature, Champion Fircot L'Ballerine, an imported Miniature, owned by Mrs. Meade and handled by Ruth Burnette Sayres, did likewise at this great show.

Undoubtedly the most exciting Poodle development of the '40's was the change in status of Toy Poodles to Poodles (Toy), thus making them officially a *Poodle,* the smallest members of the breed but judged on the same standard with the same type requisites. Now the way was clear for interbreeding between Toys and Miniatures and the establishment of Toy Poodles as we know them today.

Many experienced dog people have commented on the Poodle (Toy) as the modern miracle of the world of purebred dogs, for breeders worked knowledgeably and well to create little dogs so close to perfection and so breathtakingly beautiful that it was really incredible to contemplate the short length of time all this had involved. Both in Great Britain and in America the rush was on to breed superior Toys, with, in this writer's opinion, the American size limit being the more difficult to breed within; 10″ while the British allow 11″. I hasten to add, however, that the British have bred many a great one of less than 10-inch height as have we, and a number of these superb little dogs have come to the States where they have impressed by their size within our own limitations as well as by their beauty of balance and type.

Harmo Kennels' exciting Ch. Harmo Gay Prospector winning Best in Show at Ravenna Kennel Club, August 1968. William Trainor, handling and Charles F. Hamilton, judge.

Ch. Blakeen Bali Hai, an important Standard Poodle of the early 1950's. Handled by Bob Gorman for owners, Puttencove Kennels, Mr. and Mrs. George Putnam. Mrs. Sherman R. Hoyt, judge.

Ch. Top Hills Trumps, Miniature Poodle owned by Mrs. Gardner Cassatt, winning Best in Show from Len Carey *(center)* at Ox Ridge Kennel Club 1957. Anne Rogers Clark, handler.

One of the exciting things to happen with Poodles (Toy) was the development of all the lovely colors. Early Toy Poodles had been almost always white. But before we knew it, after the change in classification, we had gorgeous blacks, silvers, creams, apricots, browns—in fact the entire range of Poodle colors.

It almost seemed, during the '40's, that those former favorites, the Standard Poodles, were taking a back seat to the Miniatures and to the new additions, the Toys! At the Interstate Specialty of 1940 a Miniature Poodle *for the first time ever in the United States* won a Specialty Best of Breed. Monty of Gilltown, the winner, was a black dog by Sparkle of Mannerhead; he was an English import belonging to Mrs. P.H.B. Frelinghuysen, for whom Walter Morris handled.

Two years later Ramoneur of Catawba, Mrs. Austin's lovely dog, achieved his win of Best Non-Sporting dog at Westminster, another Miniature first. The following year the elegant black bitch, Champion Pitter Patter of Piperscroft, again brought home exciting honors when she became the first Miniature Poodle Westminster Best in Show. This was another owned by Mrs. Frelinghuysen and handled by Mr. Morris. Ramoneur and Pitter Patter were both descended from Chieveley Chopstick.

World War II, of course, took its toll of the dog show world as it did in everything. Shows either were discontinued entirely or took place under restricted circumstances. But when it was all over, Poodles and their owners were set to go, ready for whatever competition might have to offer.

Many Poodle greats appeared during the 1950's, some of them far too memorable ever to be forgotten. Such a dog was Champion Puttencove Promise, Best in Show at Westminster in 1958, who was owned by Mr. and Mrs. George Putnam and handled by Bob Gorman. Another white Standard, Champion Alfonco v.d. Goldenen Kette, owned by Clairedale and Pennyworth Kennels and handled by Bob Forsyth, was a frequent winner, as was Champion Blakeen Bali Hai, owned and handled by Hayes Hoyt.

The 1950's saw the establishment of two great kennels featuring Miniatures. They were Dunwalke, owned by Mr. and Mrs. Clarence Dillon, and Tydel, owned by Mrs. Marguerite Tyson. Dunwalke's most widely admired Poodle was the handsome black bitch Champion Fontclair Festoon, who in 1959 became the second Miniature Poodle to win Best in Show at Westminster, where she was handled by Anne Hone Rogers, now Mrs. James Edward Clark.

Ch. Adastra Magic Fame, the noted white Miniature Poodle who won so well for Mrs. Marguerite S. Tyson, Ty-Del Kennels, back in the 1950's, winning Best In Show, Heart of America in 1957.

Marguerite Tyson gathered the finest Miniatures she could find for what she had planned to make a long-time breeding operation. Her untimely death was a sad loss to us all! Among her dogs were Champion Adastra Magic Fame, Champion Estid Ballet Dancer, and Champion Blakeen Van Aseltine in Miniatures, and Champion Blakeen Ding Ding and the homebred Champion Tydel's Dancing Doll in Toys.

The late 1950's saw the importation of that marvelous Miniature Champion Summercourt Square Dancer of Fircot, brought to the United States by Nigel Aubrey Jones. This dog was sold to Mrs. Lewis Garlick of Gaylen Kennels. He had an exciting show career under Anne Hone Rogers's handling, but his real success came as a sire with more than 61 champions to his credit, keeping him at the top of the producer lists over a long period of time.

Champion Estid Ballet Dancer was sired by Square Dancer, as was that superb dog Champion Tedwin's Top Billing, the Poodle who returned to Westminster at ten years of age to win the breed there over all the top youngsters and the approval of all the Poodle authorities present! He was bred by Ted Young, Jr., and was owned by Colonel Ernest E. Ferguson until the Colonel's death and then by Frank Sabella; and he had a stunning record of success in all parts of the United States. He was truly a once-in-a-lifetime dog!

Frank Sabella handling the great white Miniature Ch. Tedwin's Top Billing to one of his many Bests in Show. Judge here is Ken Dyer.

Ch. Alfonco v.d. Goldenen Kette, handled by Robert S. Forsyth for Clairedale and Pennyworth Kennels. Here winning the Trenton Non-Sporting Group in 1956, judged by Kathleen Staples.

Ch. Fircot L'Ballerine winning Best In Show at the Morris and Essex Kennel Club in 1957 under judge Lewis S. Worden, Ruth Burnette Sayres handling. Also shown are owner Mrs. Saunders L. Meade *(right)* and Club President Mrs. M. Hartley *(left)*.

The stunning and widely admired black Toy of the early 1960's, Ch. Carlima's J.D., with her breeder-handler Wendell J. Sammet.

The famous white Miniature, Ch. Estid Ballet Dancer, wins the Non-Sporting Group at Westminster 1961, under judge Richard Kerns. Frank Sabella handling for Colonel E.E. Ferguson.

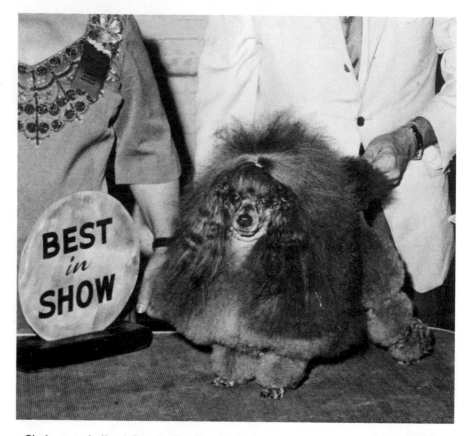

Ch. Loramar's I'm A Dandy, Toy Poodle owned by Robert D. Levy, taking Best in Show at Macon Kennel Club, April 1967.

As for the Toys of those days, of course Champion Wilbur White Swan and Champion Cappoquin Little Sister come first to mind due to their Bests in Show at Westminster in 1956 and 1961 respectively. Wendell Sammet handled one I especially liked: Champion Carlima's J.D., which he bred. And Audrey Watts Kelch had some marvelous little Toys in Champion Fieldstreams Bojangles and Champion Fieldstreams Valentine, both handled by Ben Burwell.

Then there were the Robert Levys with several really thrilling Toy winners, some of which are pictured in this book and several of which were consistent Best in Show winners. Top campaigner was the adorable brown, Champion Loramar's I'm A Dandy, whose Best in Show record grew to formidable proportions during his career.

Ch. Alekai Pokoi owned by Alekai Poodles, Mrs. Henry J. Kaiser, winning Best in Show, Kennel Club of Buffalo 1964. Dr. Wilfred Eugene Shute, judge. Wendell J. Sammet, handler.

Ch. Emmrill Lucky Charm, owned by Dunwalke Kennels, taking Best in Show from judge William L. Kendrick at Miami in 1961. William Lang, A.K.C. Representative on the *left*. Mrs. Anne Rogers Clark handling.

Lorraine Waldron's handsome black Miniature, Ch. Cavalier Poetic Justice, by Cavalier Here Comes De Judge ex Cavalier's Glory Girl, winning Best of Winners at Westminster in 1973.

The handsome Standard dog, Ch. Alekai Luau, did some mighty important winning for Ann Seranne and Barbara Wolferman a decade or so ago. Here winning Best in Show at North Shore Kennel Club, June 1970. Mr. Henry Wheeler, Jr., judge. Wendell J. Sammet, handler.

Ch. Barbree Round Dancer, owned by Miss Rosemary Breden, Glenview, Illinois, is handled here by Ruth Cooper to Best in Show at Terre Haute in 1961.

Ch. Surrey Sequoia, Top Producing brown Poodle and Top Winning Miniature of 1973 in the United States, owned by Mrs. Margaret Durney, Malibu, California.

# Chapter 4

# *American Poodles of Today*

From coast to coast, and in all sections of the United States, Poodle breeders are continuing to produce top-flight dogs, and the breed holds its own quite steadily in quality and registrations. It would be impossible to give a kennel by kennel listing here of all who deserve acclaim for their accomplishments, so we have picked just highlights to relate.

Starting with the Standards, who could possibly deny that magnificent white bitch, Champion Lou-Gin's Kiss Me Kate, the praise she deserves for the incomparable role she has played in Poodle history? This, indeed, was a once-in-a-lifetime Poodle who brought honor to her breed in keenest competition when she became America's Number One Best in Show Dog, with the winning of her 140th Best in Show, breaking the previous record by fourteen victories.

Miss Kate's entire show career was an inspiration to us all. First, she was a *bitch*—the first of her sex to attain such heights—and of a *coated* breed, about which there are always people around saying that those "never have a chance against the males." Kate disproved *that* theory in a hurry. And I must say that I never have seen her in the ring when she looked other than in flawless coat and super condition!

Champion Lou Gin's Kiss Me Kate was born on May 23rd 1976, daughter of Champion Ilex Barclay, C.D., from Champion Lou Gin's Chateau Chalon, at the Lou Gin Kennels. She was sold to Barbara and Terri Meyers, under whose ownership she started her show career as a puppy, handled by Bob Walberg.

This is the great Toy Poodle Ch. Syntifny On The Move, owned and handled by Dana L. Plonkey, Valcopy Poodles, Alderwood Manor, Washington. A son of Ch. Syntifny Piece of the Rock ex Patience of Slocum, On The Move has sired 33 champions as of March 1984, including Ch. Valcopy Dream Walking, Ch. Char-Dan Jazzman of Lynns, and Ch. Darrette's Das Es All.

**Opposite page:**
*(Top)* Ch. Syntifny On The Move, Poodle Club of America Stud Dog Class, with three of his kids: Ch. Char-Dan Jazzman of Lynns (Best in Show winner), Ch. Langcroft Ease On Down, and Ch. Char-Dan Kopy Kat of Samilee, another Best in Show winner. On The Move belongs to Dana L. Plonkey. *(Bottom)* The magnificent Standard Poodle bitch, Ch. Alekai Marlaine, handled by Wendell Sammet for Alekai Kennels, taking Best in Show at Northwestern Connecticut in 1966.

Ch. Rimskittle Ruffian with Tim Brazier on the Merv Griffin Show. Photo courtesy of Mrs. Margaret Durney, co-owner with Ed Jenner of this lovely bitch.

As Kate's potential became increasingly obvious, the Meyers decided that they would be willing to take co-ownership with Jack and Paulann Phelan, who loved her and wanted to share in her career. And so, after her first year and a half in the ring, she became owned by the Phelans and Terri, whose bitch she always remained. Jean and Bob Walberg cared for her (Terri almost always traveled with them) and Bob was her handler, the one to whom credit must go for her always flawless presentation.

On the occasion of her 140th Best in Show, Kate was retired and returned to the Meyers where it was planned she would enjoy a long life as a "family dog" and have puppies. The shock and sadness of her sudden death, of bloat, during June 1983 is indescribable! Kate was Terri Meyers's constant companion since returning home and had been asleep in Terri's room when stricken. Prompt and expert care failed to save her, and before anyone could believe what was happening, Kate was gone—such a heartbreaking loss, not only for the Meyers and the others of her "family" who had so dearly loved her but also for the Poodle breed, as Kate had already produced some lovely champions and who knows what might have been still to come? (The full story of Kate's life and career appears in *The Book of the Poodle*.)

Another great Standard bitch, the black Champion Rimskittle Ruffian, also met with a tragic death early in the 1980's after an impressive show career. Ruffian, owned during her show career by Mrs. Margaret Durney and Mr. Edward Jenner and handled so well by Timothy Brazier, won outstanding honors in all parts of the United States and at its most prestigious events. She had been retired and returned to her breeders, Mr. and Mrs. James Edward Clark, when she met with her lamentable death. It must be some solace to all concerned with Ruffian, however, that she has left an extraordinarily beautiful daughter, Champion Rimskittle Riot, whom Tim Brazier is now campaigning for Mrs. Durney.

Riot's sire, Champion Longleat Alimar Raisin Cane, is a very handsome black Standard bred and owned by Alisia Duffy; he did some spectacular winning early in the 1980's in the East and seemed destined for a long and exciting career, handled by Richard Bauer for co-owner Mrs. Gardner Cassatt. However, Alisia's interests turned away from dog shows and, as Raisin Cane was her very special dog, his career was ended. It is interesting that these two handsome blacks should have produced so fabulous a white as Riot, who certainly should follow through with a show career highly creditable to both parents!

During the late 1970's, it was Champion Rimskittle Bartered Bride who was going strong for Margaret Durney. She, too, was a Poodle of incredible beauty in the ring and was handled by Tim Brazier. She was bred by the Clarks.

Dassin Poodles, owned by Freeman C. (Bud) Dickey and Joseph Vergnetti, have been responsible for a dynasty of black Standards during the past decade or so, starting with Champion Jocelyene Marjorie, a gorgeous blue bitch, and her two litters, one by Dassin Doubting Thomas (son of Champion Wycliffe Thomas) and one by Champion Winshire's Country Gentleman. In the first litter came Champion Dassin Blue Tango O'Chalmar, a Poodle Club of America Best in Specialty Show winner. In the second litter were the famous top producing brothers, Champion Dassin Broadway Joe, Champion Dassin Sum Buddy, and Champion Dassin Debauchery, the latter two both multiple Best in Show winners. According to the Poodle Club of America listings for May 1980, Champion Dassin Debauchery was then the top living sire among Standard Poodles in America; Champion Dassin Broadway Joe was in sixth place, and Champion Dassin Sum Buddy in seventh. Need we say more?

Champion Dassin Broadway Joe sired that magnificent dog Champion Dassin Debussy, who in his turn, among numerous others, is the sire of that remarkable bitch Champion Dassin Rita La Rose who is from another noted producer, the bitch Champion Dassin Six Pac. Rita La Rose and another lovely bitch, the black Standard Champion Dassin De Lux, have been keeping the Dassin banner high in the Standard world. De Lux, like Rita, is owned by Mrs. Edward Solomon.

For several decades now, Alekai and the kennels founded on it have brought fame to white Standards. Mrs. Henry J. Kaiser is the lady behind Alekai, and Wendell J. Sammet is the gentleman in charge of the dogs and their careers. Founded on four super bitches (Champion Ivardon Winter, Champion Davdon Suma Cum Laude, Champion Davdon Captivator, and Champion Tambarine de la Fontaine), on whom the finest available white Standard dogs were used (Champion Hillendale C'est Vrai, Champion Blakeen Bali Hai, Champion Ensarr Glace, and Champion Puttencove Promise), Alekai has produced, and continues today to produce, Standard Poodles of tremendous quality. Unforgettable dogs from this kennel include Champion Alekai Marlene, a bitch of exceptional elegance and beauty; Champion Alekai Pokoi, another favorite of the author's; Champion Alekai Luau, a magnificent dog; Champion Alekai Holulaka; Champion Alekai Ami;

Ch. Hells A Blazen's Fagin's Pride, a consistent Group and Best in Show winning Toy owned by Mrs. A.C. Pearson and handled by Richard Bauer.

We are indebted to the late James Walker Trullinger, judging, for this picture of one of the *greatest* of all Poodle "greats," Ch. Summercourt Square Dancer of Fircot, whose dominance as a sire is well known. Here he was just awarded Best of Breed at the 1954 Great Lakes Poodle Club of Chicago Specialty, Anne Rogers Clark handling for Mrs. Lewis Garlick (also pictured). Club President Walter R. Quennan presents the trophy.

One of the foundation bitches at Alekai, Ch. Tambarine de la Fontaine, winning Best in Show at Somerset Hills K.C. 1961. Judge, W. Ross Proctor. Wendell J. Sammet is handling for Mrs. Henry J. Kaiser.

and so very many more. Currently Alekai is exhibiting some young dogs who many feel may be the best they have ever raised, and Mrs. Kaiser's interest in the breed continues unabated.

Who in Poodles is not familiar with Bel Tor, registered in 1953, which has earned all sorts of outstanding honors with Standards of all colors and of exceptional merit, with Miniatures (to a considerably lesser degree), and, for a while, with Toys? Mrs. Jesse Mason is a fancier who has contributed inestimably to Poodles, through the raising of quality dogs, through her excellence and popularity as a judge, and through her true dedicated *interest* in the breed.

Joy Tongue, of Acadia, is another who will go down in history as having made some very noticeable contributions to the breed. Champion Acadia Command Performance, who gained a Westminster Best in Show in the 1970's for Jo Ann Sering and Edward B. Jenner, is one of the famous Poodles bearing the Acadia prefix which is known not only in the United States but also in other countries where these dogs have played a part in breed development.

We could really continue indefinitely, but space does not permit, so let us look to the Miniatures!

There are several from the past twenty years or so who stand out in my memory. One is Rita Holloway's stunning white dog, Champion J.L.C. Critique, who twice gained the Non-Sporting Group at Westminster—the first time owned by Rita Cloutier (Mrs. Holloway) and the second time by Robert Koeppel, Paul Edwards handling on both occasions. "Tiki," a stunning little dog, was Number One Miniature in the United States for 1979 and 1980. Since his retirement, he is at home with Mrs. Holloway and is thoroughly enjoying ruling the household most graciously.

Marjorie Tranchin for many years bred and imported some stunning Miniature Poodles. Her death during the early 1980's was a sad loss to the breed, as she was still much involved with her dogs and had some top ones at that time.

An exquisite head-study by Ben Burwell of Eng., Am., Can., and Mex. Ch. Montmartre Maria Nina, one of Marjorie Tranchin's great winning Miniatures.

Ch. Camelot's Most Happy Rogue, bred and owned by Nancy and Mary Ellen Fishler, Gaithersburg, Maryland, was handled by Dennis McCoy to Best of Winners at the Lehigh Valley Poodle Club Specialty in 1981.

A Miniature who stands out in my mind as one of the best of the past couple of decades is the gorgeous apricot Champion Tiopepi Amber Tanya, imported from England, owned by Mrs. Gardner Cassatt, and handled by Richard Bauer. Mrs. Cassatt is known for her love of apricot Poodles, and she is the lady who owned and campaigned the stunning Champion Pixiecroft Sunbeam some years back.

The Aizcorbes, Aizbel Kennels, have created a line of very worthy Miniatures who continue to come up with good ones in each succeeding generation.

Joseph Vergnetti and Freeman Dickey have a black Miniature bitch, descended from Joseph's early winning Mini, creating much attention these days.

Toys have created considerable excitement, and we bring you photos, among our illustrations, of many of the best of recent decades. The breeding kennels to which we pay special tribute are Sassafras, Pamela Ingram's great line, which is no longer active; Silhou-Jette, from where Martha Jane Ablett has brought forth many splendid ones; Syntifny, with its fantastic little sire Piece of the Rock, who contributed so greatly to the breed and who was mysteriously stolen from his kennel; Hells A Blazen, behind a whole series of Best in Show Toys; Arundel; Kornel; and many others who have also done their share.

Ch. Erman's Hayfield Fever is owned by Mrs. G.K. Hooker and is handled by J. Craig Osborne.

The widely admired apricot Miniature bitch Ch. Pixiecroft Sunbeam owned by Mrs. Gardner Cassatt, winning the Group, Eastern Dog Club 1963, under highly esteemed authority Henry Stoecker. Anne Rogers Clark handling.

NON-SPORTING GROUP

Ch. Silhou-Jette's Snow Sprite, owned by Martha Jane Ablett, winning the Toy Group at the Eastern Dog Club in 1959. Wendell J. Sammet, handler. Miss Delphine McEntyre, judge.

Ch. Darrette's Das Es All, one of the breed's truly great Toys, has brought many exciting top honors to his owner Annette H. Anderson of Rexburg, Idaho, for whom he was handled by Robert Peebles. Allie has been high in the ratings systems as both a show dog and a Top Producer, is a Best in Show dog and has been Top Poodle, all Varieties, as well as Top Toy.

A special bow goes to Dana Plonkey, Valcopy Poodles, Alderwood Manor, Washington, on his having bred more than fifty champions in the three varieties of Poodles. The Valcopy dogs are represented in all sections of the country, where they command respect and admiration. I think it might be said that Dana takes particular pride in his fabulous Toy, Champion Syntifny On The Move, whom he has owned since this little dog was six months old. On The Move was bred by Jane Winne and Les Paul, and is a son of the above-mentioned Champion Syntifny Piece of the Rock ex Patience of Slocum. He is the sire of 33 champions to date, which include eight Best in Show winners and many multiple Group and Variety winners. It is certainly a singular achievement that the past three top winners in the Toy Poodle world in the past three years as we write (early 1980's) are all On The Move offspring. They are Champion Valcopy Dream Walking, Champion Chardan Jazzman of Lynns, and Champion Darette's Das Es All (who is making a spectacular record as a sire, matching his own show successes).

Can. and Am. Ch. Ma Griffe Rebel, born in 1961, was one of the famous Poodles bred and owned by Phyllis Laventhal Wolfish of Toronto. From the noted Group winning Can. Ch. Jay's Ma Griffe Sparkle, Rebel was a Best in Show winner and an American Group winner from the classes.

# Chapter 5

# *Poodles in Canada*

Poodle fanciers living in Canada have more than distinguished themselves in the world of breeding dogs, and Poodles from there have been sought to be used in breeding programs throughout North and South America, Great Britain, Europe, and Australia.

This is especially true of Standards. Both Wycliffe Kennels in western Canada (Vancouver, British Columbia) and Bibelot Kennels in eastern Canada (Toronto, Ontario) have sent famous and beautiful dogs overseas where they have been used most advantageously in an effort to improve the breed.

Wycliffe Poodles are owned by Mrs. Donald Lyle, whose champions have put her high on the list of breeders who have produced the greatest number of such titles anywhere in North America. Many great stud dogs were from this kennel, among them American and Canadian Champion Wycliffe Thomas, a multiple Best in Show winner, who had 67 champions to his credit as a sire when my *The Book of the Poodle* went to press in 1982. American, Canadian, and Mexican Champion Wycliffe Kenneth, another Best in Show winner, a son of Thomas, at that same time was only one champion behind his illustrious sire. It is eloquent comment to note that in 1980 the list of top producing Standard dogs published by the Poodle Club of America contained the names of twenty Wycliffe stud dogs.

Bibelot is owned by Miss Susan Fraser, whose great star, American, Canadian, and English Champion Bibelot's Tall, Dark and Handsome, was the first American and Canadian champion Poodle ever to go to England. There he quickly became a champion, then became England's Dog of the Year for 1966 when he earned more Best in

Show awards than any other dog of any breed there, and then put frosting on the cake when he took runner-up to Best in Show at Crufts in 1967. Tall, Dark and Handsome produced a total of 53 champions in nine countries! Another Bibelot Poodle, Champion Bibelot's Rich and Rare, was the second American and Canadian Champion to go to England and gain title there.

The very well-known judge, Mrs. Phyllis Laventhal Wolfish, has long been a Poodle breeder and has produced or imported some very special ones since she came to live in Canada. Mrs. Wolfish grew up in England, where she was involved with and interested in Poodles since childhood.

A very famous and distinguished black Miniature Poodle, Int. Ch. and O.T.Ch. Karas Bucaneer of Ma Griffe, C.D., U.D., 1960-1975, a multi-Best in Show winner, Specialty Show and Group winner was by Int. Ch. Poodhall Gus ex Can. Ch. Firebrave Honourine. Bred, owned and handled by Phyllis Laventhal Wolfish, Ma Griffe Poodles, Toronto, Ontario, Can.

Ch. Jay's Ma Griffe Silver Sparkle, silver Toy Poodle, 1968-1979, the Group winning dam of the Best in Show and American Group winner, Can. and Am. Ch. Ma Griffe Rebel. Phyllis Laventhal Wolfish, owner, Ma Griffe Poodles, Toronto, Ontario, Canada.

The noted black Miniature, Can. and Am. Ch. Ma Griffe V.I.P., C.D., 1968-1983, was by Ch. Montmartre Maxwell (Eng. Ch. Montmartre Marco Polo-Vasahope Melba) ex Ch. Ma Griffe Veronique (Ch. and O.T.Ch. Karas Bucaneer of Ma Griffe-Ch. Firebrave Honourine). Owned and shown by Phyllis Laventhal Wolfish, Toronto, Ontario.

Ch. Sudbrook Sunday Joyride, 1965-1978, was a multiple Best in Show winner, Top Toy in Canada for two consecutive years, and Top Toy Poodle for three years consecutively. An English import owned by Ma Griffe Poodles, Phyllis Laventhal Wolfish, Toronto, Ont.

She imported her first Poodle from Alida Munroe of the Firebrave Kennels, a black male Miniature named Firebrave Juba. He became a Canadian champion, but Phyllis did not continue his line for breeding.

Next came Firebrave Honourine, a beautiful small black female sent over by Mrs. Munroe in whelp to Firebrave Patapan. It was Honourine, when bred to International Champion Poodhall Gus, who gave Phyllis Wolfish the Miniature who established her Ma Griffe line. This was Canadian and American Champion Karas Bucaneer of Ma Griffe, and as Phyllis says, "I enjoyed them all very much. Superb intelligence! Many of them in the next generations became obedience champions. Lovely crisp coats, beautiful feet."

81

Ma Griffe also developed, starting in the 1950's, a line of silver Miniatures which came from the Merrymorn Kennels in England, and Mrs. Wolfish still has descendants of that line. Champion Merrymorn Tara, C.D., was her constant companion for thirteen years. Phyllis has always taken pride in the fact that her conformation champions were never left forgotten in dog pens. They always went on and enjoyed themselves in the obedience ring and then retired gracefully. Karas Bucaneer was still a star performer when he retired at thirteen, at that time living with Marjorie Parkinson who was one of Canada's leading obedience trainers.

Ch. Ma Griffe Satin Doll, at seven months is a current winner representing Phyllis Laventhal Wolfish.

Ch. Kyra's Black Magic of Ma Griffe, born in 1971 and still going strong, is the dam of Can. and Am. Ch. Ma Griffe Light Traveller. Owned and shown by Phyllis Laventhal Wolfish, Ma Griffe Poodles, Toronto, Ontario, Canada.

In the 1960's, Phyllis Wolfish again traveled to England to Montmartre Kennels for another outcross which also worked out well for her.

As for the Toys, Phyllis feels that those from the small Firebrave lines and the Toys she imported in the 1950's were her prettiest. A brother and sister, called respectively Merrymorn Bunchie and Merrymorn Mellissa, although they went over the 10″ size limit in Canada (remember, 11″ is allowed in England) worked well into the breeding program and were high stationed and elegant for their time with a very pretty eye. A very small Firebrave Miniature bred to the 11″ Merrymorn male produced the tiny black male Champion Ma Griffe Black Sprite. His daughters were introduced to the Ardynas line from England, brought over by Mr. and Mrs. Hans Brunotte; and from there Phyllis bred Canadian and American Champion Ma Griffe Light Traveller, an under 10″ Group-winning male, who in turn has produced some wonderfully typey blacks for Ma Griffe.

Canadian Champion Ma Griffe's Silver Sparkle was the dam of Canadian and American Champion Ma Griffe Rebel, a Best in Show winner and a Canadian Group winner, plus a Toy Group winner from the classes in the United States. Champion Sudbrook Sunday Joyride was Top Toy Poodle for Phyllis for three consecutive years, a multiple Best in Show winner, and twice in a row Top Toy All-Breeds.

Aust. Ch. Foxmore Show and Go, stunning Standard Poodle waiting to go in the ring. Two years ago this dog beat all the others to go Best of Breed at the 1983 R.A.S.K.C. Spring Fair. Beaten only once for Best of Breed during his career, "Paris" has been a multiple in Group and in Show winner since six months of age. Owned by Reg Delaney and Brian Williams, Orange, New South Wales, who also own the Miniatures, Aust. Ch. Friande Felicity and Aust. Ch. Jeunesse By Jove, both black Best in Show winners.

# Chapter 6

# *Poodles in Australia*

Australia has become a very active and deeply involved part of the world of purebred dogs. The bonds of friendship between that country and the United States are strengthened daily as noted judges from both countries travel back and forth fulfilling prestigious assignments. The custom now is that quite frequently Australian authorities share their knowledge when in America and American judges do likewise "down under." Many American judges have returned home with glowing accounts of the country, people, and dogs with whom they have become acquainted there, and Poodles are among the breeds which have elicited particularly glowing praise. Obviously Australian breeders have selected their foundation stock well and are using it to best advantage.

Interestingly, American fanciers have found sufficient merit in the Australian-bred dogs to have imported a number to be introduced into their own kennels, and it has worked out to their advantage. The exportation of dogs from Australia is quite brisk, as is the importation of dogs to Australia, despite the lengthy quarantine procedure for dogs going to that country.

During the early part of 1984 we are hearing good things about the Standard Poodle Australian Champion Vulcan Champagne Ovalord, brought to the Australian Fancy from the United Kingdom and proven a true asset both to the show ring and as a producer. Jean Wadner, of Jurado Standard Poodles, owns this dog. Among his progeny is a son of note, Champion Foxmore Show and Go, a three-year-old from Australian Champion Pindalee Stop The Show, whose victories include the dog Challenge Certificate and Best of Breed at the Royal Agricultural Society 1983 Spring Fair Dog Show.

Another of Ovalord's prominent offspring is Mrs. A.V. Cox's Champion Juradel Royal Champagne, who is from Vicmar's Royal Event, another import from the United Kingdom. This dog also is a three-year-old, born in 1981.

Representatives of the Vulcan Champagne bloodlines (see British chapter) have been especially successful in Australia. We note a recent purchase by Jean Lawton, whose Quattuor Poodles are predominantly white Standards, of a silver dog, Vulcan Champagne Plutarch, who will undoubtedly contribute valuably.

Champion Leander Zennith, sire of no less than 30 champions, is a famed show dog and producer owned by Mrs. Hilda MacKenzie of the Pindalee Kennels—a dog of substantial influence and highly regarded.

Another fine dog is Australian Champion Kimanjoes Star Attraction, by English Champion Kimanjoes Double Diamond of Tragapanz. Four years old, he belongs to Mrs. P.M. Ellis and Miss J. Smith.

Australian Champion Leander Show Stopper is the sire of Mrs. N. Winstanley's exciting Australian Champion Chappelle Makin Whoopee (from Australian Champion Stepout on the Hillside), who in turn sired the glamourous bitch Australian Champion Chappelle Jean Harlow, whose dam is Stepaway for Moretime and who is co-owned and handled by Erica Thomas-Howe. Erica Thomas-Howe, along with her sister, breeds Poodles and English Cockers under the Marechal prefix. Both ladies have worked closely with Mrs. Winstanley and her Chappelle Poodles in Brisbane, as well as with Margaret Emery whose Stepout and Stepaway Poodles were formerly of Melbourne and are now at Brisbane.

In 1975, together with Mrs. Hazel Baldwin, Mrs. Thomas-Howe and her sister Edwina Thomas purchased and imported the black Standard bitch Champion Leander Luck of the Draw who had been imported from the United Kingdom by J. and I. Coudray. "Lea" at that time was about eighteen months old. Not only did this gorgeous bitch become a great show dog in her own right, but she is also a top producer. Her wins include multi-Best in Show honors, with Challenge Certificates at Sydney, Brisbane, and Adelaide Royals. Her winning progeny include ten champions from only four litters. Three of them each are by Champion Leander Prowler, Champion Leander Zennith, and Champion Leander Show Stopper, all United Kingdom imports. Her tenth is by the United States import Champion Dassin

Aust. Ch. Leander Show Stopper was imported from the United Kingdom and is owned by E. Thomas and Margaret Emery, Queensland, Australia. Photo by Michael Trafford.

Aust. Ch. Chappelle Jean Harlow was by Aust. Ch. Chappelle Makin Whoopee ex Stepaway For Moretime. Owned and bred by N. Winstanley, handled and co-leased by E.M. Thomas-Howe, Northwood, Sydney, Australia.

Damien. "Lea" was bred by Roger Stone and Graham Thompson of Vanetonia Kennels. She was sired by English Champion Detonator of Leander (imported from the United States), an Executive son, out of English Champion Vicmar's Boname.

Then in 1977, Erica Thomas-Howe with her sister and with Margaret Emery imported Australian Champion Leander Show Stopper, bred by Wendy Streatfield and sired by English and American Champion Acadia Stagedoor Johnny of Leander, bred in the United States, who was a son of Champion Acadia Command Performance. Show Stopper's dam was Torpaz Mystique, a daughter of English Champion Torpaz Eskimo Nell. A Best in Show winner on four occasions, with Sydney Royal Best of Breed and Challenge Certificate to his credit, Show Stopper proceeded to put himself on the map as the sire of exceptional Poodles. His progeny include Best Puppy in Show at both the Sydney and Melbourne Royals as well as Best in Show at Brisbane Royal, these wins having been made by three different Poodles from three different litters. He has to date eleven champion children with more in the process of finishing, and they include three champions from "Lea." Show Stopper is the sire of the lovely and successful dog Champion Chappelle's Makin Whoopee and the double grandsire of Makin Whoopee's daughter Champion Chappelle Jean Harlow.

Aust. Ch. Stepout Moon Madness, multi-Best in Show winner, is daughter of Aust. Ch. Beguinette Winter Ermine (U.K. import) and the dam of Aust. Ch. Stepaway Heavenly Time. Owned and exhibited by Margaret Emery and Nola Winstanley, Queensland, Australia. Photo by Michael Trafford.

Champion Leander Luck of the Draw and Champion Leander Show Stopper, their children, and now their grandchildren have dominated the show scene in Standard Poodles throughout Australia during recent years, Erica Thomas-Howe points out, with hardly a Royal Challenge Certificate awarded in Standards to anything not descended from one or both of them.

Champion Leander Luck of the Draw and Champion Leander Show Stopper died within six months of each other in 1983. Their legacy lives on and their influence on Standard Poodles in Australia and New Zealand will be felt far into the future.

Aust. Ch. Leander Luck of the Draw, (U.K. import) is by Eng. Ch. Acadia Detonator of Leander (American import) ex Eng. Ch. Vicmar's Boname. Owned by E.M. Thomas-Howe, E.J. Thomas, and H. Baldwin. Bred by R. Stone and G. Thompson.

Dukees Ice Capade at ten weeks, by Aust. Ch. Millbrook Super Star ex Aust. Ch. Belvakees Snow Queen, is owned by Reg W. Delaney and Brian Williams, Orange, New South Wales, Australia, whose kennel features Standards and Miniatures. This Standard puppy will be starting a show career soon.

Chappelle Shadow Play, by Am. Ch. Oakgrove Heavenly Sum Buddy (American import) ex Stepaway a Wild Flower, is here winning Best of Breed and Best Minor in Group. Owned by K. Maraun and E.M. Thomas-Howe and bred by Mrs. N. Winstanley.

Chappelle Wish Me Wines, by Aust Ch. Chappelle Making Whoopee ex Chapelle Curtain Call, is owned and handled by Nola Winstanley, Queensland, Australia.

S.D. Thomas owns a very worthy Standard bitch in Marsden Best N Broadway, daughter of Champion Dassin Damien ex Marechal Star Turn. Three years old, she is a littermate to the handsome dog Australian Champion Marsden Broadway Night owned by J.A. Edwards and P.W. Warburton.

Miniatures keep themselves well in the Australian Poodle limelight. One of the notable Miniatures is Champion Beritas Back In Town, a multiple Best in Show winner and an importation from the United Kingdom. Neil Fitzgerald of the Matchabelli Kennels is the owner of this lovely Poodle.

Elysee Kennels have an admired producer in Champion Elysee the Hustler, who is the sire of New Zealand Champion Marsden Tom Foolery. Rhonda Berg Phillips owns Elysee Poodles. Tom Foolery belongs to J.A. Edwards and P.W. Warburton. Another dog who is becoming well known carrying the Elysee prefix is Elysee Hustle N Bustle, a fifteen-month-old youngster who took Reserve Challenge in Miniatures at the Royal Agricultural Society 1983 Spring Fair. Owners of this one are C.F. and L.G. Wright.

Troy Tanner, we note, won Best of Breed in *both* Miniatures and Toys at the Spring Fair, proof that his truly magnificent Poodles are continuing along their successful ways. In Miniatures it was Hades Bad Habits, co-owned with L. Henery, a just-past-year-old son of Australian Champion Troymere Man About Town ex Hades Cantstop The Music who carried off the dog Challenge Certificate and Best of Breed. In Toys it was High Wings High Voltage, imported from the United States, a daughter of American Champion Sundown Sassafras Bootblack ex American Champion High Winds Luv N Stuf, who took the bitch Challenge Certificate and Best of Breed.

We note some fine kennels specializing in Toys in the New South Wales area. They include Sunbeam Kennels, where black Toys are featured by Marea Ireland, owner of the well-known stud dog Champion Sunbeam The Wizard. Wizard puppies have been winning firsts at the Royals and include Australian Champion Sunbeam Mister Niceguy, from Australian Champion Kerita Crowning Glory, owned by J. and Mrs. R.J. Boot.

T. and L. Neve specialize in apricot and black Toys at Trelor Kennels. Bob and Pat Gray have the Loire black Toys, founded on English bloodlines. Australian Champion Loire Liberty Belle is from this kennel, as is the young dog Loire Nicen Naughty (by Australian Champion Cherarna Black Classic ex Francelle Fleur Delys) and

Aust. Ch. Elysee Bliss, Miniature Poodle by Aust. Ch. Elysee The Hustler ex Aust. Ch. Elysee Hell's Belle. This Best Miniature Poodle at the Sydney Royal is owned by Mrs. Rhonda Berge Phillips, Lohengrin, Dural, Australia.

Vulcan Champagne Plutarch in December 1983. This silver male by Silver Trapper of Whittens ex Vulcan Champagne Pandora, was bred by Miss A.C. Coppage who exported him to Australia, to Mrs. J. Lawton, in 1983.

A very important Miniature Poodle from Australia, Ch. Elysee The Hustler, by Aust. Ch. Marsden Happy Talk ex Carmoquist Anna Michelle (U.K. import). At just over four years of age has been Reserve Challenge Dog under Anne Rogers Clark; Best of Breed under Keke Blumberg; and Best Puppy in Show at the Poodle Club Championship Show under English judge Vicky Marshall (Vicmar Poodles). Sire of ten champions including Best of Breed at the Sydney Royal under Anne Clark, and Best of Breed at the Melbourne Royal under Maxine Beam. Bred and owned by Mrs. R. Berge Phillips, Lohengrin, Dural, Australia.

Loire Sweet Charity (Australian Champion Semloh Witch Doctor ex Liberty Belle). Mrs. Norma Oakey, of Springmead, is another Toy breeder specializing in blacks. Hers include Champion Loire Toucho Class, Reserve Best of Breed at the Spring Fair 1983, and some nice winning puppies to watch for in the future. Mrs. M. Demunster at

Aust. Ch. Elysee Bliss with some of her trophies. This lovely daughter of Aust. Ch. Elysee The Hustler was bred and is owned by Mrs. R. Berge Phillips, Dural, Australia. Best Miniature Poodle at the Sydney Royal under Anne Rogers Clark.

Liegeois Poodles breeds white and black Toys, as does Mrs. P. Kemp at Casjo Kennels.

Veteran Poodle breeders in the New South Wales area are John Edwards and Philip Warburton, who started with English Cockers in 1960 and shortly thereafter established the Marsden Poodles, where all three varieties are featured. The background of the Marsden Toys was a little black champion, Barsbrae Outward Bound, who was imported from England by Mr. Edwards in partnership with a friend and who at the time my *The Book of the Poodle* (in which these kennels are

Aust. Ch. Marsden Mindya Manners, handsome winning Standard Poodle owned by J. Edwards and P. Warburton, Glenorie, New South Wales, Australia.

fully reviewed) was written in 1981 had already sired more than 50 Australian champions.

Marsden's first Miniature, purchased by Mr. Edwards and Mr. Warburton, was Champion Jeunesse Justa Joie, son of the well-known British sire of the 1970's, English Champion Tranchant Philisma. Joie produced five champions and was joined at the kennel by other importations from the United Kingdom, including Australian Champion Beritas Bianco, also a producer of five champions. Then, from the United States, came English and American Champion Black Delinquent of Idatown, top winning Miniature of her time in Australia and producer of at least half a dozen champions, among them a daughter, Champion Marsden Black Antics, Best of Breed at various of the Royals as has been another daughter, Champion Marsden Black Dilemma.

To start them out in Standards, Marsden purchased a bitch from Wycliffe and Acadia strains, Champion Tandonia A Touch of Spice, who has numerous Challenge Certificates from the Royals. A litter-sister to this bitch has proven a superb producer as the dam of Champion Marsden Mindya Manners and Champion Marsden Doubting Thomas, both leading winners.

Troy Tanner, Troymere Kennels, had two Miniature and four Toy Poodles when he arrived in Australia during 1974 and surely lost no time in becoming a breeder of note of both these varieties. A stunning chocolate Toy, Champion Montmartre Marmion of Montfleuri, from the United Kingdom was one of the foundation bitches; another, Champion Francelle My Felicity, Australian-born, was a quality Toy stud. They were bred to give Troy Tanner Champion Troymere's Achievement and Champion Troymere's The Way We Were in successive litters, and these two full sisters have made Toy history with important wins at the Royals.

Top Ch. L'ambre Fire Bird, son of Am. and Jap. Ch. Kornel Keeper of the Kastle, winning Best Puppy in Show at the Tokyo International All-Breed event. Handled by Miyako Fukazawa. Bred and owned by Mr. and Mrs. Yukichi Fukazawa, L'ambre Poodles, Fujinomiya, Japan.

# Chapter 7

# *Poodles in Japan and South Africa*

## *Japan*

We use L'ambre Kennels as an example of what is taking place in Japan as their efforts have succeeded so well.

It was in 1969 that Mr. and Mrs. Yukichi Fukazawa of Fujinomiya City, Shizuoa, Japan, discovered Poodles and were so completely charmed by the breed, particularly the delightful Toy variety, that they decided they would enjoy breeding and raising them. Very sensibly, they felt that the best way to go about it would be to visit the United States to meet the breeders and see what dogs they felt would make suitable foundation stock for the high quality kennel they were planning. So in June 1970 they spent a month in the United States, having arranged to do so at a time which could include their attendance at the Poodle Club of America Specialty Show.

The trip was both memorable and successful, for during it the Fukazawas became acquainted with Mrs. Judith Feinberg, owner of Arundel Toys, whose dogs were to become so valuable a part of the L'ambre breeding program. By the time of their return home, the Fukazawas had succeeded in purchasing several Arundel Poodles which they planned to combine in their basic breeding program.

These little dogs were Champion Arundel A Lovin Spoonful, Champion Arundel Shine Little Star, and Champion Arundel Splash O'Dash. The results of combining these lines with those of the Hilltop dogs they already owned have more than fulfilled the Fukazawas' highest hopes and expectations.

Trips to the United States were made again in 1975 and in 1977. During one of these, the Fukazawas became impressed with the progeny of that marvelous dog Champion Syntifny's Piece of the Rock. His bloodlines came to L'ambre through Champion Kornel's Keeper of the Kastle—again a successful and fortunate purchase!

Both Lovin Spoonful and Keeper of the Kastle have made impressive records as show dogs; but, most important of all to their owners, they have become truly notable producers and by now one or both are to be found behind the leading winners from L'ambre.

Throughout the 1970's, L'ambre Poodles dominated the Specialty shows held by the Tokyo Kennel Club in Japan—very significant, as Specialty shows are the highlights of the year which bring out the finest dogs from all kennels.

Jap. Ch. L'ambre The Super Star, by Jap. Ch. L'ambre Grand Prix (son of Am. and Jap. Ch. Arundel A Lovin Spoonful) ex Jap. Ch. L'ambre Kiss The Sun (daughter of Am. and Jap. Ch. Kornel Keeper of the Kastle). Best in Show winner and Japan's 1983 Number One Poodle, here winning at the Hamamatsu Kennel Club Show, K. Igarashi, judge. Bred and owned by Mr. and Mrs. Yukichi Fukazawa, L'ambre Poodles, Fujinomiya, Japan.

Japanese Ch. L'ambre Thunder Bird is a Best in Show winner, and was Number Three Toy Poodle male in Japan, *Promotion News System,* for 1983. A son of Am. and Jap. Ch. Kornel Keeper of the Kastle, is here taking Best in Show, November 13th 1983, Tokyo Kennel Club Championship Dog Show, under judge K. Sugahara. Owned by the world famous L'ambre Poodles, Mr. and Mrs. Yukichi Fukazawa, Fujinomiya, Japan.

Now the success has continued into the 1980's, with some handsome descendants of the original dogs continuing the winning for which L'ambre has gained such wide acclaim.

Champion L'ambre The Super Star, Number One Poodle in Japan for 1983 and an all-breed and Specialty Best in Show winner, is by Champion L'ambre Grand Prix (a son of Lovin Spoonful), who was himself the 1976 Specialty Best of Breed. Super Star's dam is from Champion L'ambre Kiss The Sun, who is the daughter of Keeper of the Kastle. Ch. L'ambre Fire Bird is by Keeper of the Kastle from Champion L'ambre Lovely June. Champion L'ambre Thunder Bird, a Best in Show winner during 1983 and Number Three Toy Poodle in Japan, is a son of Keeper.

The poodles mentioned here are just a few examples of what the Fukazawas have accomplished as breeders through their enthusiasm and dedication to Toy Poodles!

Jap. Ch. L'ambre The Super Star is also a perfect show dog, as one notes how beautifully this little Poodle poses on his own. One of the many outstanding Toy Poodles bred and owned by Mr. and Mrs. Yukichi Fukazawa in Japan.

## *South Africa*

We understand that the foremost Poodle breeders in South Africa are the Browning sisters, Jacqui and Francesca, who breed all three varieties. These two ladies have spent their entire lifetime in the fancy and are actually second generation fanciers as their parents were both leading judges. Unfortunately, their mother passed away not long ago, but their dad is still alive, well, and continuing to officiate at the shows.

The Brownings are at Lombardy East in Johannesburg.

The South African dog show world is another which has grown considerably during recent years. Friends from the United States who have judged there speak well of the quality of the dogs in many breeds. To gain a championship in that country a dog must earn five points by earning Challenge Certificates, which may be for either one or two points depending on the number of entries. A judge reserves the right to withhold a Challenge Certificate if he considers the dogs in competition to be inferior.

Am., Can., Italian, Spanish, and F.C.I. (Belgium) Int. Ch. Parrish Souvenir Sue with handler Robert N. Peebles. At this time Sue had, additionally, two of the three certificates needed in France, two of four in the Netherlands, and one of two in Monaco. Owned by Lt. Col. James M. Parrish, Universal City, Texas.

**Robert N. Peebles, handler, with the famous Group and Best in Showing winning Toy Ch. Anjone China Collier, who was Top Toy Poodle in the United States for 1978. Bred and owned by Marcelle Rhoades.**

106

# Chapter 8

# *Poodle Standards*

## *American Standard*

The following Poodle standard, developed by the Poodle Club of America, was approved by the American Kennel Club on February 14th 1978. In the United States, Standard and Miniature Poodles are granted championship status in the Non-Sporting Group and Toy Poodles compete in the Toy Group.

GENERAL APPEARANCE, CARRIAGE AND CONDITION: That of a very active, intelligent and elegant-appearing dog, squarely built, well proportioned, moving soundly and carrying himself proudly. Properly clipped in the traditional fashion and carefully groomed, the Poodle has about him an air of distinction and dignity peculiar to himself. HEAD AND EXPRESSION: (a) *Skull:* Moderately rounded, with a slight but definite stop. Cheekbones and muscles flat. Length from occiput to stop about the same as length of muzzle. (b) *Muzzle:* Long, straight and fine, with slight chiseling under the eyes. Strong without lippiness. The chin definite enough to preclude snipiness. Teeth white, strong, and with a scissors bite. (c) *Eyes:* Very dark, oval in shape and set far enough apart and positioned to create an alert intelligent expression. (d) *Ears:* Hanging close to the head, set at or slightly below eye level. The ear leather is long, wide, and thickly feathered; however, the ear fringe should not be of excessive length.
NECK AND SHOULDERS: Neck well proportioned, strong and long enough to permit the head to be carried high and with dignity. Skin snug at throat. The neck rises from strong, smoothly muscled

shoulders. The shoulder blade is well laid back and approximately the same length as the upper foreleg.

BODY: To insure the desirable squarely-built appearance, the length of body measured from the breastbone to the point of the rump approximates the height from the highest point of the shoulders to the ground. (a) *Chest:* Deep and moderately wide with well sprung ribs. (b) *Back:* The topline is level, neither sloping nor roached, from the highest point of the shoulder blade to the base of the tail, with the exception of a slight hollow just behind the shoulder. The loin is short, broad, and muscular.

TAIL: Straight, set on high and carried up, docked of sufficient length to insure a balanced outline.

LEGS: (a) *Forelegs:* Straight and parallel when viewed from the front. When viewed from the side the elbow is directly below the highest point of the shoulder. The pasterns are strong. Bone and muscle of both forelegs and hindlegs are in proportion to size of dog. (b) *Hindlegs:* Straight and parallel when viewed from the rear. Muscular with width in the region of the stifles which are well bent; femur and tibia are about equal in length; hock to heel short and perpendicular to the ground. When standing, the rear toes are only slightly behind the point of rump. The angulation of the hindquarters balances that of the forequarters.

FEET: The feet are rather small, oval in shape with toes well arched and cushioned on thick firm pads. Nails short but not excessively shortened. The feet turn neither in nor out. Dewclaws may be removed.

COAT: (a) *Quality:* (1) curly—of naturally harsh texture, dense throughout. (2) corded—hanging in tight even cords of varying length; longer on mane or body coat, head, and ears; shorter on puffs, bracelets, and pompons. (b) *Clip:* A Poodle under 12 months may be shown in the "Puppy" clip. In all regular classes, Poodles 12 months or over must be shown in the "English Saddle" or the "Continental" clip. In the Stud Dog and Brood Bitch classes and in a non-competitive Parade of Champions, Poodles may be shown in the "Sporting" clip. A Poodle shown in any other type of clip shall be disqualified. (1) "Puppy" —A Poodle under a year old may be shown in the "Puppy" clip with the coat long. The face, throat, feet and base of the tail are shaved. The entire shaven foot is visible. There is a pompon on the end of the tail. In order to give a neat appearance and a smooth unbroken line, shaping of the coat is permissible. (2) "English Saddle"—In the "English Saddle" clip, the face, throat, feet, forelegs and base of the tail are shaved, leaving puffs on the forelegs and a pompon on the end of the

Ch. Dassin De Lux, one of Mrs. Edward Solomon's noted winners, relaxing a bit while waiting to go in the ring.

tail. The hindquarters are covered with a short blanket of hair except for a curved shaved area on each flank and two shaved bands on each hindleg. The entire shaven foot and a portion of shaven leg above the puff are visible. The rest of the body is left in full coat but may be shaped in order to insure overall balance. (3) "Continental"—In the "Continental" clip, the face, throat, feet, and base of the tail are shaved. The hindquarters are shaved with pompons (optional) on the hips. The legs are shaved leaving bracelets on the hindlegs and puffs on the forelegs. There is a pompon on the end of the tail. The entire shaven foot and a portion of the shaven foreleg above the puff are visible. The rest of the body is left in full coat but may be shaped in order to insure overall balance. (4) "Sporting"—In the "Sporting" clip, a Poodle shall be shown with face, feet, throat, and base of tail shaved, leaving a scissored cap on the top of the head and a pompon on the end of the tail. The rest of the body and legs are clipped or scissored to follow the outline of the dog, leaving a short blanket of coat no longer than one

Mrs. Henry J. Kaiser's Ch. Alekai All Together was Best Puppy (insert) at the 1979 Specialty Show of the Watchung Mountain Poodle Club. Then the following year returned to take Best of Breed there under judge Merrill Cohen and was also Best of Winners, from the 12-18 months class, at the Poodle Club of America Specialty in 1980.

inch in length. The hair on the legs may be slightly longer than that on the body.

In all clips the hair of the topknot may be left free or held in place by no more than three elastic bands. The hair is only of sufficient length to present a smooth outline.

COLOR: The coat is an even and solid color at the skin. In blues, grays, silvers, browns, cafe-au-laits, apricots, and creams the coat may show varying shades of the same color. This is frequently present in the somewhat darker feathering of the ears and in the tipping of the ruff. While clear colors are definitely preferred, such natural variation in the shading of the coat is not to be considered a fault. Brown and cafe-au-lait Poodles have liver-colored noses, eye-rims and lips, dark toenails and dark amber eyes. Black, blue, gray, silver, cream and white Poodles have black noses, eye-rims and lips, black or self-colored toenails, and very dark eyes. In the apricots while the foregoing coloring is preferred, liver-colored noses, eye-rims and lips, and amber eyes are permitted but are not desirable.

GAIT: A straightforward trot with light springy action and strong hindquarters drive. Head and tail carried up. Sound effortless movement is essential.

SIZE: The Standard Poodle is over 15 inches at the highest point of the shoulders. Any Poodle which is 15 inches or less in height shall be disqualified from competition as a Standard Poodle.

The Miniature Poodle is 15 inches or under at the highest point of the shoulders, with a minimum height in excess of 10 inches. Any Poodle which is over 15 inches or is 10 inches or less at the highest point of the shoulders shall be disqualified from competition as a Miniature Poodle.

The Toy Poodle is 10 inches or under at the highest point of the shoulders. Any Poodle which is more than 10 inches at the highest point of the shoulders shall be disqualified from competition as a Toy Poodle.

### VALUE OF POINTS

General appearance, temperament, carriage and condition . . . . . . . .30
Head, expression, ears, eyes and teeth . . . . . . . . . . . . . . . . . . . . . . . .20
Body, neck, legs, feet and tail . . . . . . . . . . . . . . . . . . . . . . . . . . . . . .20
Gait . . . . . . . . . . . . . . . . . . . . . . . . . . . . . . . . . . . . . . . . . . . . . . . . . . .20
Coat, color and texture . . . . . . . . . . . . . . . . . . . . . . . . . . . . . . . . . . .10

TOTAL     100

## MAJOR FAULTS

Any distinct deviation from the desired characteristics described in the Breed Standard with particular attention to the following:

*Temperament:* Shyness or sharpness.

*Muzzle:* Undershot, overshot, wry mouth, lack of chin.

*Eyes:* Round, protruding, large or very light.

*Pigment:* Color of nose, lips and eye rims incomplete, or of wrong color for color of dog.

*Neck and Shoulders:* Ewe neck, steep shoulders.

*Tail:* Set low, curled, or carried over the back.

*Hindquarters:* Cow hocks.

*Feet:* Paper or splayfoot.

## DISQUALIFICATIONS

*Clip:* A dog in any type of clip other than those listed under Coat shall be disqualified.

*Parti-colors:* The coat of a parti-colored dog is not an even solid color at the skin but of two or more colors. Parti-colored dogs shall be disqualified.

*Size:* A dog over or under the height limits specified shall be disqualified.

## British and Australian Standards

The British standards for the three Poodle varieties are the same as the Australian standards, and all three varieties of this breed are granted championship status in the Utility Group of Non-Sporting breeds.

### Poodle (Standard)

CHARACTERISTICS AND GENERAL APPEARANCE: That of a very active, intelligent, well balanced and elegant looking dog with good temperament, carrying himself very proudly.

GAIT: Sound, free movement and light gait are essential.

HEAD AND SKULL: Long and fine with slight peak at the back. The skull not broad and with a moderate stop. Foreface strong and well chiselled, not falling away under the eyes; bones and muscle flat. Lips tight fitting. Chin well defined but not protruding. The whole head must be in proportion to the size of the dog.

EYES: Almond shaped, dark, not set too close together, full of fire and intelligence.

Vulcan Champagne Soloist, shown at fourteen months old, a stunning black bitch by Quartzo Midnight Encore ex Wycliffe Yeowoman of Vulcan (Canadian import). Homebred, owned by Miss A.C. Coppage, Vulcan Kennels, Taunton, Somerset, England.

EARS: The leather long and wide, low set on, hanging close to the face.

MOUTH: Teeth white, strong, even, with scissor bite. A full set of 42 teeth is desirable.

NECK: Well proportioned, of good length and strong to admit of the head being carried high and with dignity. Skin fitting tightly at the throat.

FOREQUARTERS: Shoulders strong and muscular, sloping well to the back, legs set straight from the shoulders, well muscled.

BODY: Chest deep and moderately wide. Ribs well sprung and rounded. Back short, strong, slightly hollowed, loins broad and muscular.

HINDQUARTERS: Thighs well developed and muscular, well bent stifles, well let down hocks, hind legs turning neither in nor out.

FEET: Pasterns strong, tight feet proportionately small, oval in shape, turning neither in nor out, toes arched, pads thick and hard, well cushioned.

TAIL: Set on rather high, well carried at a slight angle away from the body, never curled or carried over the back, thick at the root.

COAT: Very profuse and dense of good harsh texture without knots or tangles. All short hair close, thick and curly. It is strongly recommended that the traditional lion clip be adhered to.

COLOUR: All solid colours. White and cream Poodles to have black nose, lips and eyerims, black toenails desirable. Brown Poodles to have dark amber eyes, dark liver nose, lips, eyerims, and toenails. Apricot Poodles to have dark eyes with black points or deep amber eyes with liver points. Black, silver and blue Poodles to have black nose, lips, eyerims and toenails. Cream, apricot, brown, silver and blue Poodles may show varying shades of the same colour up to 18 months. Clear colours preferred.

SIZE: 38 cm (15″) and over.

FAULTS: Heavy build, clumsiness, long back, snipy in foreface, light or round or prominent eyes, lippiness, bad carriage, heavy gait, coarse head, over or undershot or pincer mouth, flesh coloured nose, coarse legs and feet, long flat toes, open soft coats with no curl, particolours—(white markings on black or coloured Poodles, lemon or other markings on white Poodles), vicious temperament.


**Poodle (Miniature)**

The Poodle (Miniature) should be in every respect a replica, in miniature, of the Standard Poodle. Height at shoulder should be under 38 cm (15″) but not under 28 cm (11″).

## Poodle (Toy)

The standard of the Poodle (Toy) is the same as that of the Poodle (Standard) and Poodle (Miniature) except that the height at shoulder should be under 28 cm (11″).

Aust. Ch. Foxmore Comin' On Strong, by Aust. Ch. Leander Zennith (U.K. import) ex Aust. Ch. Pindalee Stop The Show, owned by W. and E. Burton, Australia. A multi-all-breed Best in Show winner, including under American judges Mr. and Mrs. Ward, this Poodle is also Best of Breed at Spring Fair Show under noted Poodle specialist Miss Maxine Beam and has many in-Group and in-Show awards to his credit.

Exchange of greetings! Ch. Rimskittle Bartered Bride says "hi" to the famous Bichon, "Banjo."

# Chapter 9

# *Poodle Popularity and Versatility*

Why are Poodles so popular? Why do they so consistently retain this popularity? Why is it that once having owned a Poodle few people can bear ever to be without one? There have to be reasons, and there are—lots of them.

To begin with, there is the obvious matter of size. Whether you like a tiny dog, a small dog, a medium-sized dog, or a big dog, there stands the Poodle! What other breed can offer a size range from "teacup" to sporting dog?

Then there is color. I know people who can't stand white dogs ("too much trouble always bathing them"), people who adore white dogs, those who would never want other than a black dog, some who dote on silvers, and others who think the cream to brown shades are exquisite. No matter where your feeling may lie in this matter, you will find a Poodle color to please you, plus the added asset of a coat that does not shed and does not normally cause allergies even though you may have that problem with other breeds.

Because of the many differences in size, a Poodle to suit your household is never hard to find. If you are one who likes to travel, spend weekends away from home and take your dog with you, what could be better than a Toy Poodle, light and easy to carry when necessary, even to smuggle into your room should furtive measures be necessary to get it there, quiet and never a nuisance? Also, if you live in a small apartment and have limited space, or if you are a career person who must sometimes be away for longer-than-usual days, a Toy Poodle can have

Ch. Onno Nay's Toyopet winning the Toy Group at Trenton Kennel Club in May 1961. The judge is Mrs. Emma Haug. Mrs. Ann Stevenson is handling for owners Jim and Harriet Orton.

plenty of exercise for its size just roaming the apartment; and being small, it can use a paper for toilet emergencies, if you have had the forethought to train it that way. This relieves you of the feeling that you *must* rush home to get the dog out.

A Toy or a Miniature Poodle makes the ideal city pet. They are sophisticated little dogs who love people, and they are seldom timid, as are some dogs, shrinking from crowds and traffic. Your Poodle enjoys going with you; our own Miniature only regrets that so many shops now are "out of bounds" to dogs, as she loved nothing better than to accompany us to such places. Poodles are quiet and mannerly and not given to excessive barking, causing you problems with even the friendliest of neighbors.

As for the Standards, they are a perfect suburban or country dog, offering many of the assets of a sporting breed (remember that they were originally developed as such). There are people who feel that the Standards are the nicest, steadiest, and most sensible of *all* the Poodles. They are certainly dogs who are pleasant to have around: clean, intelligent, and hardy.

Actually, all sizes of Poodles are hardy. Cared for properly, they should lead a long and happy, carefree life, which is definitely on the plus side considering how fond one is apt to become of a canine family member.

Note the gorgeous head and eye of this famous and exquisite white Standard Poodle bitch, Ch. Alekai Marlaine, one of the early homebred winners from Alekai Kennels, Mrs. Henry J. Kaiser. Mrs. Sherman R. Hoyt is here making the Best in Show award, one of many, to Marlaine. Wendell J. Sammet handling.

Ch. Tranchant Man To Man, one of Marjorie Tranchin's many outstanding black Miniature Poodles, so highly successful over the years.

All Poodles are intelligent, almost humanly so. They are quick to learn, have retentive memories, and are eager to please. For this reason they make wonderful dogs for obedience training and for obedience competition. Just notice, as you read this book, how many of them have obedience degrees and have also attained all of the highest available honors in this area!

Poodles are not difficult to care for, despite their coats. In the grooming chapter we have outlined for you two ways of keeping the coat with very little trouble. And we have pointed out to you the ease with which you can have them professionally groomed if they are to be show dogs or if you enjoy having yours done up in one of the latest chic clips. If you are a lady of fashion, you can change your Poodle's hair style almost as often as you do your own! Or if you prefer the more conservative, your Poodle in a Sporting clip will be easy for you to do and keep him looking conservatively handsome.

Poodles are an easy dog if you are considering raising the breed. They do not run into whelping difficulties, as do many of the big-headed, more massive breeds, and Caesareans are seldom necessary. The bitches also make very good mothers, caring for their babies with gentleness and concern.

If you are thinking of the breed to show, they are always impressive in the ring, and of course Poodles over the years have done a large percentage of Best in Show and Group winning. They do need to be properly turned out to be shown successfully; but depending on your feelings in the matter, it is fun to place the dog in charge of a handler; or if you prefer doing things yourself, there is the challenge to attend a grooming school, take the dog to show training classes, and teach *yourself* to become an expert.

The larger Poodles are nice pets for children, in fact among the very nicest. Toy Poodles, or small Miniatures, may be a bit fragile for a young child as they could too easily be injured by thoughtlessly rough handling; but a Standard, gentle and sensible, is second to none in patience and understanding and devotion.

Poodles are not fighters, and they get along amicably with other pets. They also love riding in cars (they don't shed all over the upholstery) and romping over the countryside with you. All in all, they are superb dogs and ownership of one is bound to be a pleasant, happy association provided you are a person who loves and enjoys the companionship of a devoted canine.

Ch. Anjone China Collier as a puppy. Famous Best in Show, Group, and Specialty Best in Show winner owned by Marcelle Rhoades and handled by Robert N. Peebles.

# Chapter 10

# *The Purchase of Your Dog or Puppy*

Careful consideration should be given to what breed of dog you wish to own prior to your purchase of one. If several breeds are attractive to you, and you are undecided which you prefer, learn all you can about the characteristics of each before making your decision. As you do so, you are thus preparing yourself to make an intelligent choice; and this is very important when buying a dog who will be, with reasonable luck, a member of your household for at least a dozen years or more. Obviously since you are reading this book, you have decided on the breed—so now all that remains is to make a good choice.

It is never wise to just rush out and buy the first cute puppy who catches your eye. Whether you wish a dog to show, one with whom to compete in obedience, or one as a family dog purely for his (or her) companionship, the more time and thought you invest as you plan the purchase, the more likely you are to meet with complete satisfaction. The background and early care behind your pet will reflect in the dog's future health and temperament. Even if you are planning the purchase purely as a pet, with no thoughts of showing or breeding in the dog's or puppy's future, it is essential that if the dog is to enjoy a trouble-free future you assure yourself of a healthy, properly raised puppy or adult from sturdy, well-bred stock.

Throughout the pages of this book you will find the names and locations of many well-known and well-established kennels in various areas. Another source of information is the American Kennel Club (51 Madison Avenue, New York, New York 10010) from whom you can obtain a list of recognized breeders in the vicinity of your home. If you plan to have your dog campaigned by a professional handler, by all means let the handler help you locate and select a good dog. Through their numerous clients, handlers have access to a variety of interesting show prospects; and the usual arrangement is that the handler re-sells the dog to you for what his cost has been, with the agreement that the dog be campaigned for you by him throughout the dog's career. I most strongly recommend that prospective purchasers follow these suggestions, as you thus will be better able to locate and select a satisfactory puppy or dog.

Your first step in searching for your puppy is to make appointments at kennels specializing in the chosen breed, where you can visit and inspect the dogs, both those available for sale and the kennel's basic breeding stock. You are looking for an active, sturdy puppy with bright eyes and intelligent expression and who is friendly and alert; avoid puppies who are hyperactive, dull, or listless. The coat should be clean and thick, with no sign of parasites. The premises on which he was raised should look (and smell) clean and be tidy, making it obvious that the puppies and their surroundings are in capable hands. Should the kennels featuring the breed you intend owning be sparse in your area or not have what you consider attractive, do not hesitate to contact others at a distance and purchase from them if they seem better able to supply a puppy or dog who will please you *so long as it is a recognized breeding kennel of that breed*. Shipping dogs is a regular practice nowadays, with comparatively few problems when one considers the number of dogs shipped each year. A reputable, well-known breeder wants the customer to be satisfied; thus he will represent the puppy fairly. Should you not be pleased with the puppy upon arrival, a breeder such as I have described will almost certainly permit its return. A conscientious breeder takes real interest and concern in the welfare of the dogs he or she causes to be brought into the world. Such a breeder also is proud of a reputation for integrity. Thus on two counts, for the sake of the dog's future and the breeder's reputation, to such a person a *satisfied* customer takes precedence over a sale at any cost.

If your puppy is to be a pet or "family dog," I feel the earlier the age at which it joins your household the better. Puppies are weaned and ready to start out on their own, under the care of a sensible new owner, at about six weeks old; and if you take a young one, it is often easier to train it to the routine of your household and your requirements of it than is the case with an older dog which, even though still a puppy

Aust. Ch. Chappelle Sensation going Best Puppy in Show, Toowoomba Royal.

Ch. Alekai Aledar, son of Ch. Alekai Brilliance, litter sister to Ch. Alekai All Together, belongs to Mr. and Mrs. Robert Shade in Eagle, Idaho, for whom he is handled by Wendell J. Sammet.

126

technically, may have already started habits you will find difficult to change. The younger puppy is usually less costly, too, as it stands to reason the breeder will not have as much expense invested in it. Obviously, a puppy that has been raised to five or six months old represents more in care and cash expenditure on the breeder's part than one sold earlier and therefore should be and generally is priced accordingly.

There is an enormous amount of truth in the statement that "bargain" puppies seldom turn out to be that. A "cheap" puppy, cheaply raised purely for sale and profit, can and often does lead to great heartbreak including problems and veterinarian's bills which can add up to many times the initial cost of a properly reared dog. On the other hand, just because a puppy is expensive does not assure one that is healthy and well reared. I know of numerous cases where unscrupulous dealers have sold for several hundred dollars puppies that were sickly, in poor condition, and such poor specimens that the breed of which they were supposedly members was barely recognizable. So one cannot always judge a puppy by price alone. Common sense must guide a prospective purchaser, plus the selection of a *reliable*, well-recommended dealer whom you know to have well satisfied customers or, best of all, a specialized breeder. You will probably find the fairest pricing at the kennel of a breeder. Such a person, experienced with the breed in general and with his or her own stock in particular, through extensive association with these dogs has watched enough of them mature to have obviously learned to assess quite accurately each puppy's potential—something impossible where such background is non-existent.

One more word on the subject of pets. Bitches make a fine choice for this purpose as they are usually quieter and more gentle than the males, easier to house train, more affectionate, and less inclined to roam. If you do select a bitch and have no intention of breeding or showing her, by all means have her spayed, for your sake and for hers. The advantages to the owner of a spayed bitch include avoiding the nuisance of "in season" periods which normally occur twice yearly, with the accompanying eager canine swains haunting your premises in an effort to get close to your female, plus the unavoidable messiness and spotting of furniture and rugs at this time, which can be annoying if she is a household companion in the habit of sharing your sofa or bed. As for the spayed bitch, she benefits as she grows older because this simple operation almost entirely eliminates the possibility of breast cancer ever occurring. I personally believe that all bitches should eventually be spayed—even those used for show or breeding when their careers are ended—in order that they may enjoy a happier, healthier old age. Please take note, however, that a bitch who has been spayed (or an altered dog) *cannot be shown at American Kennel Club Dog shows once this operation has been performed.* Be certain that you are *not* interested in showing her before taking this step.

Also in selecting a pet, never underestimate the advantages of an older dog, perhaps a retired show dog or a bitch no longer needed for breeding, who may be available quite reasonably priced by a breeder anxious to place such a dog in a loving home.

Everything we have said about careful selection of your pet puppy and its place of purchase applies, but with many further considerations, when you plan to buy a show dog or foundation stock for a future breeding program. Now is the time for an in-depth study of the breed, starting with every word and every illustration in this book and all others you can find written on the subject. The standard of the breed now has become your guide, and you must learn not only the words but also how to interpret them and how they are applicable in actual dogs before you are ready to make an intelligent selection of a show dog.

If you are thinking in terms of a dog to show, obviously you must have learned about dog shows and must be in the habit of attending them. This is fine, but now your activity in this direction should be increased, with your attending every single dog show within a reasonable distance from your home. Much can be learned about a breed at ringside at these events. Talk with the breeders who are exhibiting. Study the dogs they are showing. Watch the judging with concentration, noting each decision made and attempt to follow the reasoning by which the judge has reached it. Note carefully the attributes of the dogs who win and, for your later use, the manner in which each is presented. Close your ears to the ringside know-it-alls, usually novice owners of only a dog or two and very new to the Fancy, who have only derogatory remarks to make about all that is taking place unless they happen to win. This is the type of exhibitor who "comes and goes" through the Fancy and whose interest is usually of very short duration owing to lack of knowledge and dissatisfaction caused by the failure to recognize the need to learn. You, as a fancier who we hope will last and enjoy our sport over many future years, should develop indepen-

**Opposite page:** Ch. Tiopepi's Amber Tanya, a Best in Show apricot who made a big record during the 1970's for Mrs. Gardner Cassatt. Richard Bauer handling.

Ch. Jay Lee Bright Promise, a homebred owned by Mr. and Mrs. Joseph Dazzio.

dent thinking at this stage; you should learn to draw your own conclusions about the merits, or lack of them, seen before you in the ring and thus, sharpen your own judgment in preparation for choosing wisely and well.

Note carefully which breeders campaign winning dogs, not just an occasional isolated good one but consistent, homebred winners. It is from one of these people that you should select your own future "star."

If you are located in an area where dog shows take place only occasionally or where there are long travel distances involved, you will need to find another testing ground for your ability to select a worthy show dog. Possibly, there are some representative kennels raising this breed within a reasonable distance. If so, by all means ask permission of the owners to visit the kennels and do so when permission is granted. You may not necessarily buy then and there, as they may not have available what you are seeking that very day, but you will be able to see the type of dog being raised there and to discuss the dogs with the breeder. Every time you do this, you add to your knowledge. Should one of these kennels have dogs which especially appeal to you, perhaps you could reserve a show-prospect puppy from a coming litter. This is frequently done, and it is often worth waiting for a puppy.

We have already discussed the purchase of a pet puppy. Obviously this same approach applies in a far greater degree when the purchase involved is a future show dog. The only place at which to purchase a show prospect is from a breeder who raises show-type stock; otherwise, you are almost certainly doomed to disappointment as the puppy matures. Show and breeding kennels obviously cannot keep all of their fine young stock. An active breeder-exhibitor is, therefore, happy to place promising youngsters in the hands of people also interested in showing and winning with them, doing so at a fair price according to the quality and prospects of the dog involved. Here again, if no kennel in your immediate area has what you are seeking, do not hesitate to contact top breeders in other areas and to buy at long distance. Ask for pictures, pedigrees, and a complete description. Heed the breeder's advice and recommendations, after truthfully telling exactly what your expectations are for the dog you purchase. Do you want something with which to win just a few ribbons now and then? Do you want a dog who can complete his championship? Are you thinking of the real "big time" (*i.e.,* seriously campaigning with Best of Breed, Group wins, and possibly even Best in Show as your eventual goal)? Consider it all carefully in advance; then honestly discuss your plans with the breeder. You will be better satisfied with the results if you do this, as the breeder is then in the best position to help you choose the dog who is most likely to come through for you. A breeder selling a show dog is just as anxious as the buyer for the dog to succeed, and the breeder will represent the dog to you with truth and honesty. Also, this type of

**Overleaf** →
Ch. Medrie's White Shadow, by Ch. Regence Raised on Rock ex Ch. Kornel Hour To Remember. Bred and owned by Rita Holloway, Woodbury, Conn., who is handling.

COLUMBIA KNL CLUB
COLUMBIA MISSOURI
AUGUST 13 1978
BEST IN SHOW

breeder does not lose interest the moment the sale has been made but when necessary will be right there ready to assist you with beneficial advice and suggestions based on years of experience.

As you make inquiries of at least several kennels, keep in mind that show-prospect puppies are less expensive than mature show dogs, the latter often costing close to four figures, and sometimes more. The reason for this is that, with a puppy, there is always an element of chance, the possibility of its developing unexpected faults as it matures or failing to develop the excellence and quality that earlier had seemed probable. There definitely is a risk factor in buying a show-prospect puppy. Sometimes all goes well, but occasionally the swan becomes an ugly duckling. Reflect on this as you consider available puppies and young adults. It just might be a good idea to go with a more mature, though more costly, dog if one you like is available.

When you buy a mature show dog, "what you see is what you get"; and it is not likely to change beyond coat and condition which are dependent on your care. Also advantageous for a novice owner is the fact that a mature dog of show quality almost certainly will have received show ring training and probably match show experience, which will make your earliest handling ventures far easier.

Frequently it is possible to purchase a beautiful dog who has completed championship but who, owing to similarity in bloodlines, is not needed for the breeder's future program. Here you have the opportunity of owning a champion, usually in the two- to five-year-old range, which you can enjoy campaigning as a "special" (for Best of Breed competition) and which will be a settled, handsome dog for you and your family to enjoy with pride.

If you are planning foundation for a future kennel, concentrate on acquiring one or two really superior bitches. These need not necessarily be top show-quality, but they should represent your breed's finest producing bloodlines from a strain noted for producing quality, generation after generation. A proven matron who is already the dam of show-type puppies is, of course, the ideal selection; but these are

← **Overleaf:**
*(Top)* Ch. Lou Gin's Kiss Me Kate, with her handler Bob Walberg, became the Top Best in Show Dog of all time in the United States. This bitch died suddenly of bloat in 1982 while living in retirement with her owner, Terri Meyers, who co-owned her with Jack and Paulann Phelan. *(Bottom)* Ch. Valcopy Dream Walking, by Ch. Syntifny On The Move ex Valcopy Vanetta of Woodvale, bred by Dana Plonkey and Dianne Plager, is a winning Toy Poodle owned by Mrs. Margaret Durney, Malibu, California.

134

usually difficult to obtain, no one being anxious to part with so valuable an asset. You just might strike it lucky, though, in which case you are off to a flying start. If you cannot find such a matron available, select a young bitch of finest background from top producing lines who is herself of decent type, free of obvious faults, and of good quality.

Great attention should be paid to the pedigree of the bitch from whom you intend to breed. If not already known to you, try to see the sire and dam. It is generally agreed that someone starting with a breed should concentrate on a fine collection of top-flight bitches and raise a few litters from these before considering keeping one's own stud dog. The practice of buying a stud and then breeding everything you own or acquire to that dog does not always work out well. It is better to take advantage of the many noted sires who are available to be used at stud, who represent all of the leading strains, and in each case carefully to select the one who in type and pedigree seems most compatible to each of your bitches, at least for your first several litters.

To summarize, if you want a "family dog" as a companion, it is best to buy it young and raise it to the habits of your household. If you are buying a show dog, the more mature it is, the more certain you can be of its future beauty. If you are buying foundation stock for a kennel, then bitches are better, but they must be from the finest *producing* bloodlines.

When you buy a purebred dog that you are told is eligible for registration with the American Kennel Club, you are entitled to receive from the seller an application form which will enable you to register your dog. If the seller cannot give you the application form you should demand and receive an identification of your dog consisting of the name of the breed, the registered names and numbers of the sire and dam, the name of the breeder, and your dog's date of birth. If the litter of which your dog is a part is already recorded with the American Kennel Club, then the litter number is sufficient identification.

Do not be misled by promises of papers at some later date. Demand a registration application form or proper identification as described above. If neither is supplied, do not buy the dog. So warns the American Kennel Club, and this is especially important in the purchase of show or breeding stock.

Overleaf: →
Dassin de la Rose, daughter of Ch. Dassin Rita La Rose, winning Best Standard Puppy at the Poodle Club of America in 1983. Freeman Dickey handling. Owned by Mrs. Edward Solomon.

A current young "star" at Camelot Kennels, Camelot's Ice Princess, handled by Robert Fisher to a Group placement at Skyline Kennel Club in 1984. Owned and bred by Marion and Mary Ellen Fishler.

Dassin de la Rose as a puppy. This daughter of Ch. Dassin Rita La Rose is already started on a good show career. Mrs. Edward L. Solomon, breeder-owner, Pittsburgh, Pa.

# Chapter 11

# The Care of Your Puppy

## Preparing for Your Puppy's Arrival

The moment you decide to be the new owner of a puppy is not one second too soon to start planning for the puppy's arrival in your home. Both the new family member and you will find the transition period easier if your home is geared in advance for the arrival.

The first things to be prepared are a bed for the puppy and a place where you can pen him up for rest periods. I am a firm believer that every dog should have a crate of its own from the very beginning, so that he will come to know and love it as his special place where he is safe and happy. It is an ideal arrangement, for when you want him to be free, the crate stays open. At other times you can securely latch it and know that the pup is safely out of mischief. If you travel with him, his crate comes along in the car; and, of course, in travelling by plane there is no alternative but to have a carrier for the dog. If you show your dog, you will want him upon occasion to be in a crate a good deal of the day. So from every consideration, a crate is a very sensible and sound investment in your puppy's future safety and happiness and for your own peace of mind.

The crates I recommend are the wooden ones with removable side panels, which are ideal for cold weather (with the panels in place to keep out drafts) and in hot weather (with the panels removed to allow better air circulation). Wire crates are all right in the summer, but they give no protection from cold or drafts. I intensely dislike aluminum crates due to the manner in which aluminum reflects surrounding temperatures. If it is cold, so is the metal of the crate; if it is hot, the

Aust. Ch. Yasunz Amber Sun Ace, winner of more than forty Bests in Show, was the Top Dog All Breeds in 1970. This lovely dog is Nola Winstanley's special pet.

Aust. Ch. Elysee Hustle N'Bustle, by Aust. Ch. Elysee The Hustler ex Elysee Jewelled Genie, Miniature Poodle Challenge Bitch at the 1983 Brisbane Royal, is owned by Mrs. Rhonda Berge Phillips, Lohengrin, Dural, Australia.

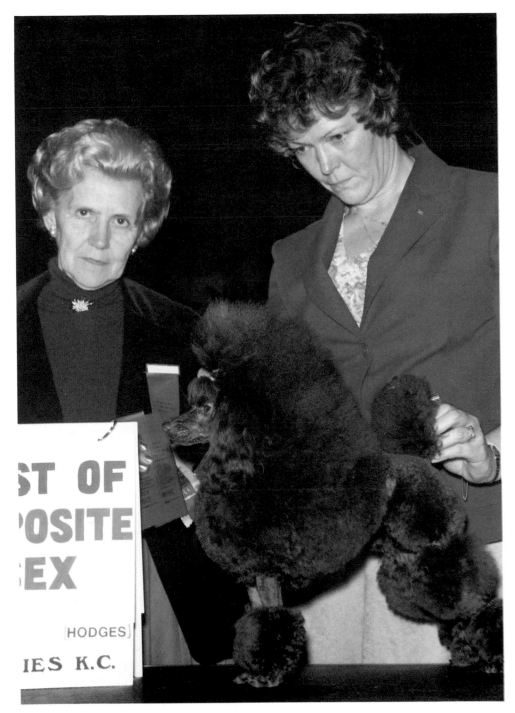

Ch. Ma Griffe Cinamon, born in 1980, from the famous bloodlines established by Phyllis Wolfish at Toronto, Ontario.

crate becomes burning hot. For this reason I consider aluminum crates neither comfortable nor safe.

When you choose the puppy's crate, be certain that it is roomy enough not to become outgrown. The crate should have sufficient height so the dog can stand up in it as a mature dog and sufficient area so that he can stretch out full length when relaxed. When the puppy is young, first give him shredded newspaper as a bed; the papers can be replaced with a mat or turkish towels when the dog is older. Carpet remnants are great for the bottom of the crate, as they are inexpensive and in case of accidents can be quite easily replaced. As the dog matures and is past the chewing age, a pillow or blanket in the crate is an appreciated comfort.

Pictured as a puppy, Aust. Ch. Beguinette Winter Ermine, imported from the United Kingdom is owned and handled by Margaret Emery, Stepaway Kennels, Queensland, Australia. She is dam of Aust. Ch. Stepout Moon Madness. Photo by Neilson.

Shown as a mature bitch, Aust. Ch. Beguinette Winter Ermine, by English Ch. Beguinette Moon River ex Beguinette Vixen. Owned and handled by Margaret Emery, Stepaway Kennels, Coopers Plains, Queensland.

Sharing importance with the crate is a safe area in which the puppy can exercise and play. If you are an apartment dweller, a baby's playpen for a toy dog or a young puppy works out well; for a larger breed or older puppy use a portable exercise pen which you can then use later when travelling with your dog or for dog shows. If you have a yard, an area where he can be outside in safety should be fenced in prior to the dog's arrival at your home. This area does not need to be huge, but it does need to be made safe and secure. If you are in a suburban area where there are close neighbors, stockade fencing works out best as then the neighbors are less aware of the dog and the dog cannot see and bark at everything passing by. If you are out in the country where no problems with neighbors are likely to occur, then regular chain-link fencing is fine. For added precaution in both cases, use a row of concrete blocks or railroad ties inside against the entire bottom of the fence; this precludes or at least considerably lessens the chances of your dog digging his way out.

**Overleaf:** →
Ch. Dassin Rita La Rose at the Poodle Club of America Specialty in 1980. Freeman Dickey handling for owner, Mrs. Edward Solomon, Pittsburgh, Pennsylvania.

BEST OF
VARIETY

POODLE CLUB
OF AMERICA
1980

GILBERT PHOTO

Be advised that if yours is a single dog, it is very unlikely that it will get sufficient exercise just sitting in the fenced area, which is what most of them do when they are there alone. Two or more dogs will play and move themselves around, but from my own experience, one by itself does little more than make a leisurely tour once around the area to check things over and then lies down. You must include a daily walk or two in your plans if your puppy is to be rugged and well. Exercise is extremely important to a puppy's muscular development and to keep a mature dog fit and trim. So make sure that those exercise periods, or walks, a game of ball, and other such activities, are part of your daily program as a dog owner.

If your fenced area has an outside gate, provide a padlock and key and a strong fastening for it, and use them, so that the gate can not be opened by others and the dog taken or turned free. The ultimate convenience in this regard is, of course, a door (unused for other purposes) from the house around which the fenced area can be enclosed, so that all you have to do is open the door and out into his area he goes. This arrangement is safest of all, as then you need not be using a gate, and it is easier in bad weather since then you can send the dog out without taking him and becoming soaked yourself at the same time. This is not always possible to manage, but if your house is arranged so that you could do it this way, I am sure you would never regret it due to the convenience and added safety thus provided. Fencing in the entire yard, with gates to be opened and closed whenever a caller, deliveryman, postman, or some other person comes on your property, really is not safe at all because people not used to gates and their importance are frequently careless about closing and latching gates *securely*. I know of many heartbreaking incidents brought about by someone carelessly only half closing a gate which the owner had thought to be firmly latched and the dog wandering out. For greatest security a fenced *area* definitely takes precedence over a fenced *yard*.

The puppy will need a collar (one that fits now, not one to be grown into) and lead from the moment you bring him home. Both should be an appropriate weight and type for his size. Also needed are a feeding dish and a water dish, both made preferably of unbreakable material. Your pet supply shop should have an interesting assortment of these and other accessories from which you can choose. Then you will need grooming tools of the type the breeder recommends and some toys. One of the best toys is a beef bone, either rib, leg, or knuckle (the latter the type you can purchase to make soup), cut to an appropriate size for

"Sam," a Miniature Poodle now long gone, photographed during happier days while enjoying his favorite Nylabone.®

your puppy dog. These are absolutely safe and are great exercise for the teething period, helping to get the baby teeth quickly out of the way with no problems. Equally satisfactory is Nylabone® , a nylon bone that does not chip or splinter and that "frizzles" as the puppy chews, providing healthful gum massage. Rawhide chews are safe, too, *IF made in the United States*. There was a problem a few years back owing to the chemicals with which some foreign rawhide toys had been treated, since which time we have carefully avoided giving them to our own dogs. Also avoid plastics and any sort of rubber toys, *particularly* those with squeakers which the puppy may remove and swallow. If you want a ball for the puppy to use when playing with him, select one of very hard construction made for this purpose and do not leave it alone with him because he may chew off and swallow bits of the rubber. Take the ball with you when the game is over. This also

A stunning headstudy of Ch. Alekai Absolute by John Ashbey. Handled by Wendell J. Sammet and owned by Mr. Gerald Silberg, Westfield, New Jersey.

Standard Poodle puppy sired by Ch. Dhubne Darth Vader, bred by Elizabeth and John Campbell.

applies to some of those "tug of war" type rubber toys which are fun when used with the two of you for that purpose but again should *not* be left behind for the dog to work on with his teeth. Bits of swallowed rubber, squeakers, and other such foreign articles can wreak great havoc in the intestinal tract—do all you can to guard against them.

Too many changes all at once can be difficult for a puppy. For at least the first few days he is with you, keep him on the food and feeding schedule to which he is accustomed. Find out ahead of time from the breeder what he feeds his puppies, how frequently, and at what times of the day. Also find out what, if any, food supplements the breeder has been using and recommends. Then be prepared by getting in a supply

← **Overleaf:**

*(Top)* Ch. L'ambre Fire Bird snapped informally. This beautiful Toy Poodle was bred and is owned by Mr. and Mrs. Yukichi Fukazawa in Japan. *(Bottom)* Japanese Ch. L'ambre The Super Star, a Best in Show winner and the 1983 #1 Poodle in Japan, here winning Best of Variety under judge Frank Sabella at the Poodle Club of Japan National Specialty Show. Owned by Mr. and Mrs. Yukichi Fukazawa.

of the same food so that you will have it there when you bring the puppy home. Once the puppy is accustomed to his new surroundings, then you can switch the type of food and schedule to fit your convenience, but for the first several days do it as the puppy expects.

Your selection of a veterinarian also should be attended to before the puppy comes home, because you should stop at the vet's office for the puppy to be checked over as soon as you leave the breeder's premises. If the breeder is from your area, ask him for recommendations. Ask your dog-owning friends for their opinions of the local veterinarians, and see what their experiences with those available have been. Choose someone whom several of your friends recommend highly, then contact him about your puppy, perhaps making an appointment to stop in at his office. If the premises are clean, modern, and well equipped, and if you like the veterinarian, make an appointment to bring the puppy in on the day of purchase. Be sure to obtain the puppy's health record from the breeder, including information on such things as shots and worming that the puppy has had.

Four generations of Deryabar Poodles: Ch. Popcorn, Ch. Ruffle, Ch. Whimsy, and puppy Flower. Owned by Mr. and Mrs. Royal Peterson, II, Greenwich, Conn.

Ch. Deryabar Whimsey with Patty Proctor, taking Winners Dog at the Watchung Mountain Poodle Club Specialty in 1980. Mr. and Mrs. Royal Peterson, II, Deryabar Poodles, Greenwich, Connecticut.

## *Joining The Family*

Remember that, exciting and happy an occasion as it is for you, the puppy's move from his place of birth to your home can be, for him, a traumatic experience. His mother and littermates will be missed. He quite likely will be awed or frightened by the change of surroundings. The person on whom he depended will be gone. Everything should be planned to make his arrival at your home pleasant—to give him confidence and to help him realize that yours is a pretty nice place to be after all.

Never bring a puppy home on a holiday. There just is too much going on with people and gifts and excitement. If he is in honor of an "occasion," work it out so that his arrival will be a few days earlier or, perhaps even better, a few days later than the "occasion." Then your home will be back to its normal routine and the puppy can enjoy your undivided attention. Try not to bring the puppy home in the evening. Early morning is the ideal time, as then he has the opportunity of getting acquainted and the initial strangeness should wear off before bedtime. You will find it a more peaceful night that way, I am sure. Allow the puppy to investigate as he likes, under your watchful eye. If you already have a pet in the household, keep a careful watch that the relationship between the two gets off to a friendly start or you may quickly find yourself with a lasting problem. Much of the future attitude of each toward the other will depend on what takes place that first day, so keep your mind on what they are doing and let your other activities slide for the moment. Be careful not to let your older pet become jealous by paying more attention to the puppy than to him, as that will start a bad situation immediately.

If you have a child, here again it is important that the relationship start out well. Before the puppy is brought home, you should have a talk with the youngster about puppies, so that it will be clearly understood that puppies are fragile and can easily be injured; therefore, they should not be teased, hurt, mauled, or overly roughhoused. A puppy is not an inanimate toy; it is a living thing with a right to be loved and handled respectfully, treatment which will reflect in the dog's attitude toward your child as both mature together. Never permit your children's playmates to mishandle the puppy, as I have seen happen, tormenting the puppy until it turns on the children in self-defense. Children often do not realize how rough is too rough.

← **Overleaf:**

This handsome black Standard is Ch. Primetime Sunday Punch owned by Mr. and Mrs. William Tow of Mt. Kisco, New York. Dennis McCoy handling, Trenton K.C. 1981.

Do not start out by spoiling your puppy. A puppy is usually pretty smart and can be quite demanding. What you had considered to be "just for tonight" may be accepted by the puppy as "for keeps." Be firm with him, strike a routine, and stick to it. The puppy will learn more quickly this way, and everyone will be happier at the result. A radio playing softly or a dim night light are often comforting to a puppy as it gets accustomed to new surroundings and should be provided in preference to bringing the puppy to bed with you—unless, of course, you intend him to share the bed as a permanent arrangement

## Socializing and Training Your New Puppy

Socialization and training of your puppy should start the very day of his arrival in your home. Never address him without calling him by name. A short, simple name is the easiest to teach as it catches the dog's attention quickly, so avoid elaborate call names. Always address the dog by the same name, not a whole series of pet names.

Using his name clearly, call the puppy over to you when you see him awake and wandering about. When he comes, make a big fuss over him for being such a good dog. He thus will quickly associate the sound of his name with coming to you and a pleasant happening.

Several hours after the puppy's arrival is not too soon to start accustoming him to the feel of a light collar. He may hardly notice it; or he may struggle, roll over, and try to rub it off his neck with his paws. Divert his attention when this occurs by offering a tasty snack or a toy (starting a game with him) or by petting him. Before long he will have accepted the strange feeling around his neck and no longer appear aware of it. Next comes the lead. Attach it and then immediately take the puppy outside or otherwise try to divert his attention with things to see and sniff. He may struggle against the lead at first, biting at it and trying to free himself. Do not pull him with it at this point; just hold the end loosely and try to follow him if he starts off in any direction. Normally his attention will soon turn to investigating his surroundings if he is outside or you have taken him into an unfamiliar room in your house; curiosity will take over and he will become interested in sniffing around the surroundings. Just follow him with the lead slackly held until he seems to have completely forgotten about it; then try with gentle urging to get him to follow you. Don't be rough or jerk at him; just tug gently on the lead in short quick motions (steady pulling can become a battle of wills), repeating his name or try-

**Overleaf:** →
Ch. Rimskittle Riot, white Standard bitch, winning the Group at Lompac Valley Kennel Club. Tim Brazier handling for Mrs. Margaret Durney, Malibu, California.

ing to get him to follow your hand which is holding a bite of food or an interesting toy. If you have an older lead-trained dog, then it should be a cinch to get the puppy to follow along after *him*. In any event, the average puppy learns quite quickly and will soon be trotting along nicely on the lead. Once that point has been reached, the next step is to teach him to follow on your left side, or heel. Of course this will not likely be accomplished all in one day but should be done with short training periods over the course of several days until you are satisfied with the result.

During the course of house training your puppy, you will need to take him out frequently and at regular intervals: first thing in the morning directly from the crate, immediately after meals, after the puppy has been napping, or when you notice that the puppy is looking for a spot. Choose more or less the same place to take the puppy each time so that a pattern will be established. If he does not go immediately, do not return him to the house as he will probably relieve himself the moment he is inside. Stay out with him until he has finished; then be lavish with your praise for his good behavior. If you catch the puppy having an accident indoors, grab him firmly and rush him outside, sharply saying "No!" as you pick him up. If you do not see the accident occur, there is little point in doing anything except cleaning it up, as once it has happened and been forgotten, the puppy will most likely not even realize why you are scolding him.

With a small or moderate size breed, especially if you live in a big city or are away many hours at a time, having a dog that is trained to go on paper has some very definite advantages. To do this, one proceeds pretty much the same way as taking the puppy outdoors, except now you place the puppy on the newspaper at the proper time. The paper should always be kept in the same spot. An easy way to paper train a puppy if you have a playpen for it or an exercise pen is to line the area with newspapers; then gradually, every day or so, remove a section of newspaper until you are down to just one or two. The puppy acquires the habit of using the paper; and as the prepared area grows smaller, in the majority of cases the dog will continue to use whatever paper is still available.

The puppy should form the habit of spending a certain amount of time in his crate, even when you are home. Sometimes the puppy will do this voluntarily, but if not it should be taught to do so, which is accomplished by leading the puppy over by his collar, gently pushing him inside, and saying firmly "Down" or "Stay." Whatever expression you use to give a command, stick to the very same one each time for each act. Repetition is the big thing in training—and so is association with what the dog is expected to do. When you mean "Sit" always say exactly that. "Stay" should mean *only* that the dog should remain where he receives the command. "Down" means something else again. Do not confuse the dog by shuffling the commands, as this will create training problems for you.

As soon as he has had his immunization shots, take your puppy with you whenever and wherever possible. There is nothing that will build a self-confident, stable dog like socialization, and it is extremely important that you plan and give the time and energy necessary for this whether your dog is to be a show dog or a pleasant, well-adjusted family member. Take your puppy in the car so that he will learn to enjoy riding and not become carsick as dogs may do if they are infrequent travelers. Take him anywhere you are going where you are certain he will be welcome: visiting friends and relatives (if they do not have housepets who may resent the visit), busy shopping centers (keeping him always on lead), or just walking around the streets of your town. If someone admires him (as always seems to happen when we are out with puppies), encourage the stranger to pet and talk with him. Socialization of this type brings out the best in your puppy and helps him to grow up with a friendly outlook, liking the world and its inhabitants. The worst thing that can be done to a puppy's personality is to overly shelter him.

## *Feeding Your Dog*

Time was when providing nourishing food for our dogs involved a far more complicated procedure than people now feel is necessary. The old school of thought was that the daily ration must consist of fresh beef, vegetables, cereal, egg yolks, and cottage cheese as basics with such additions as brewer's yeast and vitamin tablets on a daily basis.

During recent years, however, many minds have changed regarding this procedure. We still give eggs, cottage cheese, and supplements to the diet, but the basic method of feeding dogs has changed; and the change has been, in the opinion of many authorities, definitely for the

**Overleaf** →
Champion Alekai All Together, one in the long series of outstanding Standard Poodles bred at Mrs. Henry J. Kaiser's famed kennel. Handled by Wendell J. Sammet.

Ch. Dhubne Darth Vader with one of his kids. Owned by Carroll Ann Irwin and Arthur W. Mycoff.

better. The school of thought now is that you are doing your dogs a favor when you feed them some of the fine commercially prepared dog foods in preference to your own home-cooked concoctions.

The reason behind this new outlook is easily understandable. The dog food industry has grown to be a major one, participated in by some of the best known and most respected names in the American way of life. These trusted firms, it is agreed, turn out excellent products, so people are feeding their dog food preparations with confidence and the dogs are thriving, living longer, happier, and healthier lives than ever before. What more could we want?

There are at least half a dozen absolutely top-grade dry foods to be mixed with broth or water and served to your dog according to directions. There are all sorts of canned meats, and there are several kinds of "convenience foods," those in a packet which you open and dump out into the dog's dish. It is just that simple. The "convenience" foods are neat and easy to use when you are away from home, but generally speaking we prefer a dry food mixed with hot water or soup and meat. We also feel that the canned meat, with its added fortifiers, is more beneficial to the dogs than the fresh meat. However, the two can be alternated or, if you prefer and your dog does well on it, by all means use fresh ground beef. A dog enjoys changes in the meat part of his diet, which is easy with the canned food since all sorts of beef are available (chunk, ground, stewed, and so on), plus lamb, chicken, and even such concoctions as liver and egg, just plain liver flavor, and a blend of five meats.

There also is prepared food geared to every age bracket of your dog's life, from puppyhood on through old age, with special additions or modifications to make it particularly nourishing and beneficial. Our grandparents, and even our parents, never had it so good where the canine dinner is concerned, because these commercially prepared foods are tasty and geared to meeting the dog's gastronomic approval.

Additionally, contents and nutrients are clearly listed on the labels, as are careful instructions for feeding just the right amount for the size, weight, and age of each dog.

With these foods we do not feel the addition of extra vitamins is necessary, but if you do there are several kinds of those, too, that serve as taste treats as well as being beneficial. Your pet supplier has a full array of them.

Of course there is no reason not to cook up something for your dog if you would feel happier doing so. But it seems to us unnecessary

162

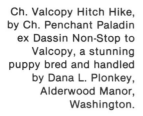
Ch. Valcopy Hitch Hike, by Ch. Penchant Paladin ex Dassin Non-Stop to Valcopy, a stunning puppy bred and handled by Dana L. Plonkey, Alderwood Manor, Washington.

when such truly satisfactory rations are available with so much less trouble and expense.

How often you feed your dog is a matter of how it works out best for you. Many owners prefer to do it once a day. I personally think that two meals, each of smaller quantity, are better for the digestion and more satisfying to the dog, particularly if yours is a household member who stands around and watches preparations for the family meals. Do not overfeed. That is the shortest route to all sorts of problems. Follow directions and note carefully how your dog is looking. If your dog is overweight, cut back the quantity of food a bit. If the dog looks thin, then increase the amount. Each dog is an individual and the food intake should be adjusted to his requirements to keep him feeling and looking trim and in top condition.

From the time puppies are fully weaned until they are about twelve weeks old, they should be fed four times daily. From three months to six months of age, three meals should suffice. At six months of age the puppies can be fed two meals, and the twice daily feedings can be continued until the puppies are close to one year old, at which time feeding can be changed to once daily if desired.

If you do feed just once a day, do so by early afternoon at the latest and give the dog a snack, or biscuit or two, at bedtime.

Remember that plenty of fresh water should always be available to your puppy or dog for drinking. This is of utmost importance to his health.

163

Ch. Camelot's The Fall Guy owned by the Fishlers, handled by Dee Shepherd, taking Winners Dog at Lehigh Valley 1983.

Some final touches before the judging. Robert N. Peebles checking that every hair is in place as an assistant keeps a steadying hand on Ch. Doral's Viking The Magician. Dorothy S. Kenck owns this handsome dog.

← **Overleaf:**
Ch. Dassin Jimmy Durante, by Ch. Dassin Dilly By Dali ex Dassin Country Pride, with Freeman Dickey.

# Chapter 12

# Your Poodle's Coat and Grooming

The breed standard for the Poodle gives a very specific description of the manner in which a show Poodle coat must be clipped. The patterns are exact, and any deviation is considered a disqualification. You will note the Puppy clip, which is legal until the puppy reaches one year's age, and the Sporting clip in which Poodles may be shown *only* in the non-competitive Parade of Champions at Specialty shows or as the sire or dam in the Stud Dog and Brood Bitch Classes.

Putting a Continental or English Saddle clip on a Poodle is a job for the professional. No inexperienced amateur ever should attempt to do it on his own until the time has come when that person no longer is inexperienced with Poodles and when that experience has taken him or her well beyond the "amateur" classification. My sincere recommendation to *all* new Poodle owners, or those just becoming exhibitors, is that they take their Poodle to a professional to have the grooming job done for the show ring once their dog is beyond the Puppy clip stage. To say that show grooming of a Poodle is *easy* is one of the largest misstatements of all time! This is pure whistling in the dark, as the plain truth of the matter is that Poodle grooming is a very complex and specialized art, requiring practice, expertise, and a very thorough knowledge of both handling a coat and the anatomy of the breed. The appearance of a show dog quite literally can be made or broken depending on whether the grooming is done by an expert or simply bungled through by an unskilled beginner. Putting a pattern on a Poo-

**Overleaf:** →
Ch. Blue Heron Silver Reprise handled by Dennis McCoy for Janet R. Madison, pictured here taking Best of Winners at Carroll K.C., 1982.

A handsome Poodle now retired to being a "family dog." The brown Standard Ch. Teller's Never Say Dye, by Ch. Teller's Levade's Final Notice ex Ch. Sangueree Solitaire, was bred by Janice Teller, Aileen Tobias, and Janet Cook, and was finished by Janice Teller with Elizabeth Campbell showing him to two 5-point majors. Primarily the Campbells' breeding, with the addition of Bel Toy and Darkin on the brown side of the family, Never Say Dye is owned by Janice Teller and the Robert L. McDills, Mission Viejo, California.

dle for the first time is extremely difficult, no matter what you may have heard or believed to the contrary.

For those readers who are seriously planning to become Poodle breeders, and to learn everything about Poodle care, I refer you to my *The Book of the Poodle* for which the famous professional handler Wendell Sammet prepared a most detailed, explicit, and enlightening chapter on the subject of clipping and grooming Poodles. It is outstandingly well done and helpful and can serve well as a guide to a person who has been involved with Poodles for awhile. We do *not*, however, advise a novice who has not spent time with Poodles and in the study of them, to blithely set out to clip or put a pattern on a dog, beyond the comparatively easy Puppy or Sporting clips.

If you have a young show dog about ready to be put into adult clip, make an appointment with a Poodle handler or someone *in the habit of grooming Poodles for the show ring* to have the job done for you. Possibly you can arrange to watch the procedure (which would be helpful for the future), but sometimes groomers prefer not to have an audience. If you really are anxious to do your own trimming, perhaps it would be a smart idea for you to enroll in one of the various dog grooming schools which are available around various cities; in that way you could learn the basics and the correct procedure. But do *not* handicap your show dog with an amateurish clip as he starts his show career!

Your Poodle, even as a puppy, should be kept brushed, tangle free, and clean. Brushing will usually suffice unless something unexpected has occurred; but if your puppy *needs* a bath, do not hesitate to give him one, using comfortably warm water and seeing that he is *thoroughly* rinsed and dried.

The Poodle family dog should be brushed at least every few days with a pin brush and combed with a steel comb, one in which the teeth are about an inch long and rather coarsely placed. A fine comb is inappropriate as it will not go through the coarse Poodle hair. The dog will need to be clipped about every six weeks to two months, depending on the growth rate of his coat.

Before clipping, the Poodle should be bathed, as only clean hair should be scissored or have clippers used on it. For the bath, start by thoroughly brushing the dog. Depending on his size, he should be bathed in a bathtub, a washtub, or a basin. Before wetting him down, place a drop of castor oil in each eye as a precautionary measure against soap reaching the eye, and place a wad of cotton in each ear to protect against water reaching the ear canal.

170

You should have a rubber shampoo spray attached to the faucet to use on the dog. Wet him down; then run a line of one of the good dog shampoos along the top of his back. Work this down into the coat by squeezing the hair with your hands, *not* by rubbing or massage which will cause tangles. Lather the dog well, rinse, and if necessary repeat the soaping. In rinsing, use your spray and be absolutely certain to do a thorough job, carefully going over every inch of the dog so as to leave no traces of the shampoo to cause skin irritation and itching. Thorough, complete rinsing is one of the most important aspects of the dog's bath. You may wish to use a cream rinse or conditioner, in which case do so according to directions and then rinse again with clear water.

When the bath is completed, squeeze as much water as you can from the coat with your hands; then blot it with a turkish towel. Do not rub with the towel, but use it as one would use blotting paper, as rubbing to dry the coat again can cause tangling.

Every Poodle owner should invest in a rubber-topped grooming table, for even with the simplest Poodle coat style, frequent grooming is necessary; and it will be far easier and more pleasant if right from puppyhood the dog is trained to stand, lie down, or stretch out on either side on one of these tables. They are non-skid for the dog due to the ribbed rubber topping, and they are compact and easily stored as the legs fold down flat when not in use. It is especially handy to also purchase an adjustable "arm" to be attached to the table; from this arm dangles a "noose" to slip over the dog's head to hold him steady while being worked on. Your Poodle will be handled in this manner when he goes for professional grooming, so it is wise to accustom him to it at home.

When the excess water has been blotted away, finish drying the moisture from the dog's coat with an electric hair dryer—your own or one especially purchased for him. As you blow-dry, brush the coat, using your pin brush, being careful to check under the forearms (arm pits), between the hind legs, and under the ears for the first sign of tangles which may form into mats. Should you find a mat, try to either brush it out gently or separate it with your fingers, trying not to hurt the dog in the process. Should more drastic measures be necessary, cut into the mat lengthwise with your scissors and then try to gently work the mat out with your comb.

A word about brushing! The correct way is to brush from the skin out, making certain that the bristles of your brush reach clear through to the skin.

Ch. Manorhill's Star of Le Aries, foundation stud belonging to Candace Mathes and Mary H. Senkowski, completed his championship with some exciting wins from the puppy classes. Under Anne Rogers Clark, he was Best Puppy in Show at the Poodle Club of America Specialty in June 1983, and also captured several other Best Puppy in Specialty awards. He was also selected for appearance in an A.K.C. slide presentation. Handled exclusively by William Cunningham.

**Opposite page:** Ch. Graphic Constellation, by Ch. Aliyah Desperado ex Ch. Graphic Helvetica, bred by Florence Graham and R. Lukens, was producer of Ch. Marney Oscar de la Renta and Ch. Marney Cacharel. Owned by Margaret Durney, Marney Kennels, Malibu, California. Constellation is here placing Winners Bitch at the Poodle Club of America Specialty in 1981. Tim Brazier handling.

Rumpelstiltskin, "Curly" to friends, America's Number One dog for 1937, looks like this after a complete beauty treatment.

To create curly rosettes on Rumpelstiltskin's legs, clipping is done carefully with special scissors.

174

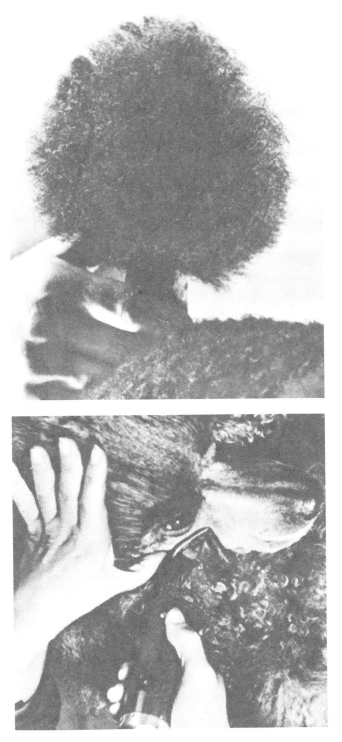

Shaving the tail requires expertise. The pom-pom at the end of the tail should measure four inches around.

Rumpelstiltskin, being a Poodle, must have his face clipped correctly to show the elegant shape of his nose. In 1937 he was entered in 51 shows and was judged to be Best of Breed 37 times.

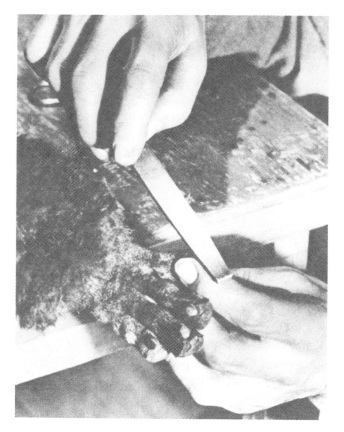

Rumpelstiltskin's toenails after clipping are next filed to smooth out any sharp or rough edges.

When your Poodle is dry, check his ears with a cotton swab dipped in peroxide to remove any excess wax and to check for signs of problems. A "smelly" ear is probably infected and should be treated by your vet. After you have checked it, then dust the ear with one of the ear powders prepared for this purpose. If hairs are growing from inside the ear (which is not unusual with heavily coated breeds), remove them with a tweezers. Done quickly, gently, and firmly, this does not hurt the dog; and this hair removal may save him considerable grief as these hairs, if permitted to remain, make an excellent base for ear mites and ear infections as wax accumulates and hardens in them.

← **Overleaf:**
Ch. Peeple's Sahara scored many a victory of Best in Show, Best Toy and won Best Toy Poodle at the Poodle Club of America Specialty on several occasions. Owned by Mr. Robert Koeppel and here handled by Richard Bauer, with judge Anna Katherine Nicholas.

If you are keeping your Poodle in Puppy or Sporting clip, it is now time to clear and shape the shaven parts and coat. For this, you should have a clipper with interchangeable heads, and you will need #15 blades and #5 blades for this type of job.

A young Poodle may be frightened by the sound of the clipper the first few times; thus he should be held *firmly* by the head to avoid any sudden lurching. This is where the "noose" comes in handy, helping to ground the dog and keep him where you need him. Start by clearing the face with the #15 blade, using a light stroke. *Do not press too hard as you may scrape the puppy's skin.* Better to go over it an extra time with a light stroke than to cause injury by being too heavy-handed. For both the Puppy and Sporting clips, the only two we are discussing here, the face and throat of the dog are cleared, the feet are shaven to about a ¼″ above where the dewclaw would be, and the base of the tail is clipped. Refer to pictures as you work, to serve as your guide. In doing the feet, use your clippers; then tidy up with scissors or shears, rounding the outline of the foot and leaving no scraggly hairs to take away from the round, tight, cat-like appearance. Clear out excess hair from between the toes, using either a curved shears or, if yours is a tiny Poodle, curved manicure scissors. The base of the tail should be clear and the tail surmounted with a pompon.

For the Puppy clip, the hair is left long as the purpose is to have it grow out sufficiently for the dog to go into an English Saddle or Continental clip for the ring. Shaping of the coat is permissible to give a smooth, neat appearance, but the shaping should be kept to a minimum.

For the Sporting clip, the coat on the body and legs is clipped (with a #5 blade) or scissored to follow the outline of the dog, making a short blanket of coat *no longer than 1″*. The hair on the legs may be slightly longer than that on the body. With this clip, there is a scissored "cap" on the top of the head, and, of course, the tail is surmounted with the pompon.

When the feet have been cleared, the toenails should be checked and shortened with either nail clippers or an electric grinder. Be careful not to cut below the quick of the nail (the pinkish line growing down a portion of the nail) as doing so will cause bleeding. Should this happen accidentally, a touch of styptic powder to the end of the nail will stop the

**Overleaf:** →
A fabulous puppy, Ch. Valcopy The Yachtsman, son of Ch. Wavir Showboat, bred and handled by Dana L. Plonkey, Alderwood Manor, Washington.

Ch. Alekai Admiration finished in four shows at eighteen months old. First time out as a Special won the Group. Bred and owned by Alekai Poodles. Handled by Wendell J. Sammet.

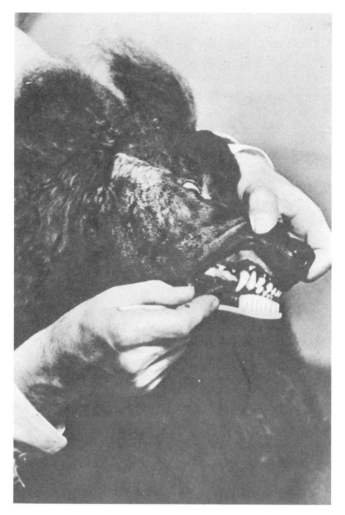

A prize Poodle's teeth should be white and are carefully cleaned regularly.

bleeding. Since the quick grows along with the nail, it is sensible to keep the latter short as then this problem will be avoided. The grinder gives the nail a smoother finish, but some dogs object violently to its use.

Your Poodle's teeth should be checked for accumulated tartar, which when seen should be removed by your veterinarian or by you with a scraper if you know how.

We feel that the foregoing formula for handling the grooming of your pet Poodle should be something everyone can manage. It will take a bit of time to perfect the art of creating a smooth and pleasing

182

outline on the coat if you have never done it before, but it is not all that difficult if you have a steady hand and eye.

There are literally dozens of patterns and manners in which Poodles coats can be clipped *if the dogs are not to be shown.* Many owners love having their dogs wear them, and the Poodles do, indeed, look chic and very stylish. Here again, though, is territory into which the amateur should not venture. Just as putting a pattern on a show dog takes expertise, so do these varied and sophisticated clips. So take your Poodle to the grooming salon for them. There are hundreds of Poodle grooming salons, which gives credence to my statement that having it done is far more satisfactory than doing it yourself. Shop around a bit if you are not pleased with the first groomer you try. There are (just as with our own hairdressers) plenty around to give one a choice, and trying one or more can be fun as they "create" something becoming to your dog. Poodles love looking smartly groomed; they seem to *know* when they look handsome and they bask in that fact.

**Overleaf:** →
Ch. Wissfire Miss Kitty, a stunning and very successful Toy Poodle of the 1970's with her handler, F.C. Dickey.

Ch. Deryabar Pirate, multiple Best in Show and Group winner, and a Top Winning Poodle in 1983. Owned by Mr. and Mrs. Royal E. Peterson, II, Deryabar, Greenwich, Conn.

← **Overleaf:**
Ch. Deryabar Trumpet, a champion at 11 months, with a Best of Variety to his credit, has gone on as a Best in Show winner. Bred by the Royal Petersons, II, Greenwich, Ct., handled by Wendell J. Sammet, he now belongs to Col. and Mrs. John Snodgrass of Newport, Rhode Island.

# Chapter 13

# The Making of a
# Show Dog

If you have decided to become a show dog exhibitor, you have accepted a very real and very exciting challenge. The groundwork has been accomplished with the selection of your future show prospect. If you have purchased a puppy, we assume that you have gone through all the proper preliminaries concerning good care, which should be the same if the puppy is a pet or future show dog with a few added precautions for the latter.

## General Considerations

Remember the importance of keeping your future winner in trim, top condition. Since you want him neither too fat nor too thin, his appetite for his proper diet should be guarded, and children and guests should not be permitted to constantly be feeding him "goodies." The best treat of all is a small wad of raw ground beef or a packaged dog treat. To be avoided are ice cream, cake, cookies, potato chips, and other fattening items which will cause the dog to put on weight and may additionally spoil his appetite for the proper, nourishing, well-balanced diet so essential to good health and condition.

The importance of temperament and showmanship cannot possibly be overestimated. They have put many a mediocre dog across while lack of them can ruin the career of an otherwise outstanding specimen.

Ch. Doral On A Dare, by Ch. Syntifny On The Move ex Syntifny Silver Sea Shell, with handler Dana L. Plonkey, Valcopy Poodles.

From the day your dog joins your family, socialize him. Keep him accustomed to being with people and to being handled by people. Encourage your friends and relatives to "go over" him as the judges will in the ring so this will not seem a strange and upsetting experience. Practice showing his "bite" (the manner in which his teeth meet) quickly and deftly. It is quite simple to slip the lips apart with your fingers, and the puppy should be willing to accept this from you or the judge without struggle. This is also true of further mouth examination when necessary. Where the standard demands examination of the roof of the mouth and the tongue, accustom the dog to having his jaws opened wide in order for the judge to make this required examination. When missing teeth must be noted, again, teach the dog to permit his jaws to be opened wide and his side lips separated as judges will need to check them one or both of these ways.

Some judges prefer that the exhibitors display the dog's bite and other mouth features themselves. These are the considerate ones, who do not wish to chance the spreading of possible infection from dog to dog with their hands on each one's mouth—a courtesy particularly appreciated in these days of virus epidemics. But the old-fashioned judges still persist in doing it themselves, so the dog should be ready for either possibility.

Take your future show dog with you in the car, thus accustoming him to riding so that he will not become carsick on the day of a dog show. He should associate pleasure and attention with going in the car, or van or motor home. Take him where it is crowded: downtown, to the shops, everywhere you go that dogs are permitted.

Do not overly shelter your future show dog. Instinctively you may want to keep him at home where he is safe from germs or danger. This can be foolish on two counts. The first reason is that a puppy kept away from other dogs builds up no natural immunity against all the things with which he will come in contact at dog shows, so it is wiser actually to keep him well up to date on all protective shots and then let him become accustomed to being among dogs and dog owners. Also, a dog who never is among strange people, in strange places, or among strange dogs, may grow up with a shyness or timidity of spirit that will cause you real problems as his show career draws near.

Keep your show prospect's coat in immaculate condition with frequent grooming and daily brushing. When bathing is necessary, use a

← Overleaf:
A famous Poodle Best in Show owned by Mrs. Solomon and handled by "Bud" Dickey is Ch. Dassin De Lux, with a quickly increasing list of Group, Best in Show and Specialty events to her credit.

Ch. McKernan Redford of Valcopy, by Ch. Wavir Showboat ex Redfern Camellia, bred by D.L. Plonkey and A. McKernan. Dana Plonkey handling, Alderwood Manor, Washington.

mild baby shampoo or whatever the breeder of your puppy may suggest. Several of the brand-name products do an excellent job. Be sure to rinse thoroughly so as not to risk skin irritation by traces of soap left behind and protect against soap entering the eyes by a drop of castor oil in each before you lather up. Use warm water (be sure it is not uncomfortably hot or chillingly cold) and a good spray. A hair dryer is a real necessity for the heavily coated breeds and can be used for thorough drying after first blotting off the excess moisture with a turkish towel. A wad of cotton in each ear will prevent water entering the ear cavity.

Formation of mats should be watched for carefully in Poodles, especially behind the ears and underneath the armpits. Toenails also should be watched and trimmed every few weeks. It is important not to permit nails to grow excessively long, as they will ruin the appearance of both the feet and pasterns.

Assuming that you will be handling the dog yourself, or even if he will be professionally handled, a few moments each day of dog show routine is important. Practice setting him up as you have seen the exhibitors do at the shows you've attended, and teach him to hold this position once you have him stacked to your satisfaction. If he is a small breed that judges examine on a table, accustom him to this. Make the learning period pleasant by being firm but lavish in your praise when he responds correctly. Teach him to gait at your side at a moderate rate on a loose lead. When you have mastered the basic essentials at home, then hunt out and join a training class for future work. Training classes are sponsored by show-giving clubs in many areas, and their popularity is steadily increasing. If you have no other way of locating one, perhaps your veterinarian would know of one through some of his other clients; but if you are sufficiently aware of the dog show world to want a show dog, you will probably be personally acquainted with other people who will share information of this type with you.

A show dog's teeth must be kept clean and free of tartar. Hard dogbiscuits can help toward this, but if tartar accumulates, see that it is removed promptly by your veterinarian. Bones are not suitable for show dogs as they tend to damage and wear down the tooth enamel.

**Opposite page:** Ch. Rimskittle Bartered Bride, by Ch. Rimskittle Right On ex Ch. Rimskittle Executant, owned by Margaret Durney, Malibu, California.

## *Match Shows*

Your show dog's initial experience in the ring should be in match show competition for several reasons. First, this type of event is intended as a learning experience for both the dog and the exhibitor. You will not feel embarrassed or out of place no matter how poorly your puppy may behave or how inept your attempts at handling may be, as you will find others there with the same type of problems. The important thing is that you get the puppy out and into a show ring where the two of you can practice together and learn the ropes.

Ch. Anjone China Collier sits in just-won trophy for Best in Show at Pensacola in 1978, as handler Robert N. Peebles smiles with pleasure. Marcelle Rhoades owns this stunning little dog.

Ch. Rimskittle Ruffian stands regally for inspection as she is judged during the finals at the Westminster Kennel Club in 1980. Mrs. Margaret Durney and Ed Jenner owners. Tim Brazier, handler.

Only on rare occasions is it necessary to make match show entries in advance, and even those with a pre-entry policy will usually accept entries at the door as well. Thus you need not plan several weeks ahead, as is the case with point shows, but can go when the mood strikes you. Also there is a vast difference in the cost, as match show entries only cost a few dollars while entry fees for the point shows may be over ten dollars, an amount none of us needs to waste until we have some idea of how the puppy will behave or how much more pre-show training is needed.

Match shows very frequently are judged by professional handlers who, in addition to making the awards, are happy to help new exhibitors with comments and advice on their puppies and their presentation of them. Avail yourself of all these opportunities before heading out to the sophisticated world of the point shows.

195

The fabulous Ch. Brown Cricket of Camelot taking a 3-point major at her very first show, the Pittsburgh Poodle Club Specialty in August 1967, handled by John Brennan for breeder-owners Nancy and Marvin Fishler. The judge is Mrs. Howard Price of England, owner of the Montfleuri black Miniatures reviewed in the English section of this book.

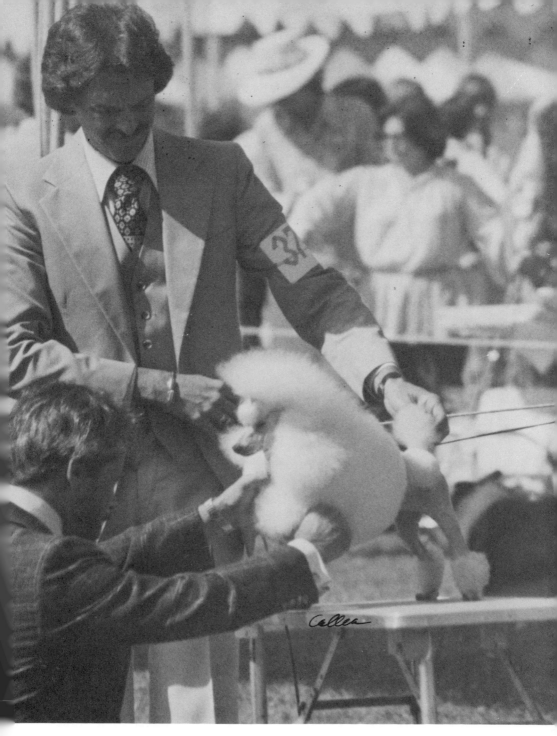

Ch. Anjone China Collier being examined by judge Edd Bivin, who is checking here for shoulder placement and correctness of forelegs.

# Point Shows

As previously mentioned, entries for American Kennel Club point shows must be made in advance. This must be done on an official entry blank of the show-giving club. The entry must then be filed either personally or by mail with the show superintendent or the show secretary (if the event is being run by the club members alone and a superintendent has not been hired, this information will appear on the premium list) in time to reach its destination prior to the published closing date or filling of the quota. These entries must be made carefully, must be signed by the owner of the dog or the owner's agent (your professional handler), and must be accompanied by the entry fee; otherwise they will not be accepted. Remember that it is not when the entry leaves your hands that counts but the date of arrival at its destination. If you are relying on the mails, which are not always dependable, get the entry off well before the deadline to avoid disappointment.

A dog must be entered at a dog show in the name of the actual owner at the time of the entry closing date of that specific show. If a registered dog has been acquired by a new owner, it must be entered in the name of the new owner in any show for which entries close after the date of acquirement, regardless of whether the new owner has or has not actually received the registration certificate indicating that the dog is recorded in his name. State on the entry form whether or not transfer application has been mailed to the American Kennel Club, and it goes without saying that the latter should be attended to promptly when you purchase a registered dog.

In filling out your entry blank, type, print, or write clearly, paying particular attention to the spelling of names, correct registration numbers, and so on. Also, if there is more than one variety in your breed, be sure to indicate into which category your dog is being entered: Standard, Miniature, or Toy.

The Puppy Class is for dogs or bitches who are six months of age and under twelve months, were whelped in the United States, and are not champions. The age of a dog shall be calculated up to and inclusive of the first day of a show. For example, the first day a dog whelped on January 1st is eligible to compete in a Puppy Class at a show is July 1st of the same year; and he may continue to compete in Puppy Classes up to and including a show on December 31st of the same year, but he is *not* eligible to compete in a Puppy Class at a show held on or after January 1st of the following year.

The great Ch. Dassin Sum Buddy, famed sire and winner owned by Freeman Dickey, snapped informally in the ring at Westminster.

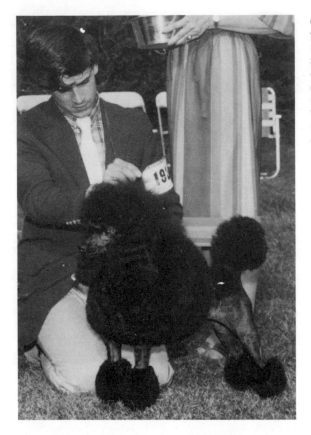

Ch. Dassin Danielle as a youngster winning Best Bred-by Exhibitor in Show at the Poodle Club of America in 1982. Owned by Freeman Dickey and Joseph Vergnetti (handling), Dassin Farm, Medina, Ohio.

The Puppy Class is the first one in which you should enter your puppy. In it a certain allowance will be made for the fact that they *are* puppies, thus an immature dog or one displaying less than perfect showmanship will be less severely penalized than, for instance, would be the case in Open. It is also quite likely that others in the class will be suffering from these problems, too. When you enter a puppy, be sure to check the classification with care, as some shows divide their Puppy Class into a 6-9 months old section and a 9-12 months old section.

The Novice Class is for dogs six months of age and over, whelped in the United States or Canada, who *prior to the official closing date for entries* have *not* won three first prizes in the Novice Class, any first prize at all in the Bred-by-Exhibitor, American-bred, or Open Classes, or one or more points toward championship. The provisions for this class are confusing to many people, which is probably the reason exhibitors do not enter in it more frequently. A dog may win any number of first prizes in the Puppy

This very attractive silver Miniature is Ch. Freeland's Faustin, by Ch. Freeland's Falstaff ex Ch. Freeland's Felicia, who finished at only nine months of age with three majors among his points. Handled by Richard Bauer for owner Dereke Jay Harvey who has been breeding dogs since 1966 at Mahopac, New York.

Class and still retain his eligibility for Novice. He may place second, third or fourth not only in Novice on an unlimited number of occasions but also in Bred-by-Exhibitor, American-bred and Open and still remain eligible for Novice. But he may no longer be shown in Novice when he has won three blue ribbons in that class, when he has won even one blue ribbon in either Bred-by-Exhibitor, American-bred, or Open, or when he has won a single championship point.

In determining whether or not a dog is eligible for the Novice Class, keep in mind the fact that previous wins are calculated according to the official published date for closing of entries, not by the date on which you may actually have made the entry. So if in the interim, between the time you made the entry and the official closing date, your dog makes a win causing him to become ineligible for Novice, change your class *immediately* to another for which he will be eligible, preferably such as either Bred-by-Exhibitor or American-bred. To do this, you must contact the show's superintendent or secretary, at first by telephone to save time and at the same time confirm it in writing. The Novice Class always seems to have the fewest entries of any class, and therefore it is a splendid "practice ground" for you and your young dog while you are getting the "feel" of being in the ring.

Bred-by-Exhibitor Class is for dogs whelped in the United States or, if individually registered in the American Kennel Club Stud Book, for dogs whelped in Canada who are six months of age or older, are not champions, and are owned wholly or in part by the person or by the spouse of the person who was the breeder or one of the breeders of record. Dogs entered in this class must be handled in the class by an owner or by a member of the immediate family of the owner. Members of an immediate family for this purpose are husband, wife, father, mother, son, daughter, brother or sister. This is the class which is really the "breeders' showcase," and the one which breeders should enter with particular pride to show off their achievements.

The American-bred Class is for all dogs excepting champions, six months of age or older, who were whelped in the United States by reason of a mating which took place in the United States.

The Open Class is for any dog six months of age or older (this is the only restriction for this class). Dogs with championship points compete in it, dogs who are already champions are eligible to do so, dogs who are imported can be entered, and, of course, American-bred dogs compete in it. This class is, for some strange reason, the favorite of exhibitors who are "out to win." They rush to enter their pointed dogs

Ch. Erman's Ace In The Hole, Winners Dog for five-points at the Poodle Club of America in 1981. Bred and owned by Mr. and Mrs. Terry Erman, Moore, Oklahoma.

in it, under the false impression that by doing so they assure themselves of greater attention from the judges. This really is not so, and in my opinion to enter in one of the less competitive classes, with a better chance of winning it and thus earning a second opportunity of gaining the judge's approval by returning to the ring in the Winners Class, can often be a more effective strategy.

One does not enter for the Winners Class. One earns the right to compete in it by winning first prize in Puppy, Novice, Bred-by-Exhibitor, American-bred, or Open. No dog who has been defeated on the same day in one of these classes is eligible to compete for Winners, and every dog who has been a blue-ribbon winner in one of them and not defeated in another, should he have been entered in more than one class, (as occasionally happens) *must* do so. Following the selection of the Winners Dog or the Winners Bitch, the dog or bitch receiving that award leaves the ring. Then the dog or bitch who placed second in that class, unless previously beaten by another dog or bitch in another class at the same show, re-enters the ring to compete against the remaining first-prize winners for Reserve. The latter award indicates that the dog or bitch selected for it is standing "in reserve" should the one who received Winners be disqualified or declared ineligible through any technicality when the awards are checked at the American Kennel Club. In that case, the one who placed Reserve is moved up to Winners, at the same time receiving the appropriate championship points.

Winners Dog and Winners Bitch are the awards which carry points toward championship with them. The points are based on the number of dogs or bitches actually in competition, and the points are scaled one through five, the latter being the greatest number available to any one dog or bitch at any one show. Three-, four-, or five-point wins are considered majors. In order to become a champion, a dog or bitch must have won two majors under two different judges, plus at least one point from a third judge, and the additional points necessary to bring the total to fifteen. When your dog has gained fifteen points as described above, a championship certificate will be issued to you, and your dog's name will be published in the champions of record list in the *Pure-Bred Dogs/American Kennel Gazette,* the official publication of the American Kennel Club.

The scale of championship points for each breed is worked out by the American Kennel Club and reviewed annually, at which time the number required in competition may be either changed (raised or lowered) or remain the same. The scale of championship points for all breeds is published annually in the May issue of the *Gazette,* and the current ratings for each breed within that area are published in every show catalog.

When a dog or bitch is adjudged Best of Winners, its championship points are, for that show, compiled on the basis of which sex had the greater number of points. If there are two points in dogs and four in bitches and the dog goes Best of Winners, then *both* the dog and the bitch are awarded an equal number of points, in this case four. Should the Winners Dog or the Winners Bitch go on to win Best of Breed or Best of Variety, additional points are accorded for the additional dogs and bitches defeated by so doing, provided, of course, that there were entries specifically for Best of Breed Competition or Specials, as these specific entries are generally called.

Ch. Bentwater Aztec, owned by Jean Bray, Braewyns Kennels, taking Winners Dog en route to his title at the Quinnipiac Poodle Club in 1974.

If your dog or bitch takes Best of Opposite Sex after going Winners, points are credited according to the number of the same sex defeated in both the regular classes and Specials competition. If Best of Winners is also won, then whatever additional points for each of these awards are available will be credited. Many a one-or two-point win has grown into a major in this manner.

Moving further along, should your dog win its Variety Group from the classes (in other words, if it has taken either Winners Dog or Winners Bitch), you then receive points based on the greatest number of points awarded to any member of any breed included within that Group during that show's competition. Should the day's winning also include

Best Brace in Show at Chicago-International in 1969. The Miniature Poodles Ch. Top Brass of Gladgay and Ch. Challenger of Gladgay owned by Mr. and Mrs. Kenneth Hanna, Framingham, Mass. Jane Forsyth handling, Percy Roberts judge.

Best in Show, the same rule of thumb applies, and your dog or bitch receives the highest number of points awarded to any other dog of any breed at that event.

Best of Breed competition consists of the Winners Dog and the Winners Bitch, who automatically compete on the strength of those awards, in addition to whatever dogs and bitches have been entered specifically for this class for which champions of record are eligible. Since July 1980, dogs who, according to their owner's records, have completed the requirements for a championship after the closing of entries for the show, but whose championships are unconfirmed, may be transferred from one of the regular classes to the Best of Breed competition, provided this transfer is made by the show superintendent or show secretary *prior to the start of any judging at the show.*

This has proved an extremely popular new rule, as under it a dog can finish on Saturday and then be transferred and compete as a Special on Sunday. It must be emphasized that the change *must* be made *prior* to the start of *any* part of the day's judging, not for just your individual breed.

In the United States, Best of Breed winners are entitled to compete in the Variety Group which includes them. This is not mandatory, it is a privilege which exhibitors value. (In Canada, Best of Breed winners *must* compete in the Variety Group, or they lose any points already won.) The dogs winning *first* in each of the seven Variety Groups *must* compete for Best in Show. Missing the opportunity of taking your dog in for competition in its Group is foolish as it is there where the general public is most likely to notice your breed and become interested in learning about it.

Non-regular classes are sometimes included at the all-breed shows, and they are almost invariably included at Specialty Shows. These include Stud Dog Class and Brood Bitch Class, which are judged on the basis of the quality of the two offspring accompanying the sire or dam. The quality of the latter two is beside the point and should not be considered by the judge; it is the youngsters who count, and the quality of *both* are to be averaged to decide which sire or dam is the best and most consistent producer. Then there is the Brace Class (which, at all-breed shows, moves up to Best Brace in each Variety Group and then Best Brace in Show), which is judged on the similarity and evenness of appearance of the two members of the brace. In other words, the two dogs should look like identical twins in size, color, and conformation and should move together almost as a single dog, one person handling

Poodle Club of America, Autumn 1982. Stud Dog Class: Ch. Syntifny On The Move, sire; Ch. Poco Poco Front and Center; and Ch. Valcopy On The Town, Best of Variety. On The Move owned by Dana L. Plonkey, Valcopy Poodles, Alderwood Manor, Washington.

Ch. Clairlac Calaban of Foxfire, a Group and Specialty Best in Show winner, handled by Robert N. Peebles for owner, William H. Williams, Jr., Foxfire Kennels.

Ch. Lime Crest Topper with owner-handler Bob Levy winning Best in Show under Melbourne Downing at Clearwater Kennel Club, January 1961.

with precision and ease. The same applies to the Team Class competition, except that four dogs are involved and, if necessary, two handlers.

The Veterans Class is for the older dogs, the minimum age of whom is seven years. This class is judged on the quality of the dogs, as the winner competes in Best of Breed competition and has, on a respectable number of occasions, been known to take that top award. So the point is *not* to pick out the oldest dog, as some judges seem to believe, but the best specimen of the breed, exactly as in the regular classes.

Then there are Sweepstakes and Futurity Stakes sponsored by many Specialty clubs, sometimes as part of their regular Specialty Shows and sometimes as separate events on an entirely different occasion. The difference between the two stakes is that Sweepstakes entries usually include dogs from six to eighteen months age with entries made at the same time as the others for the show, while for a Futurity the entries are bitches nominated when bred and the individual puppies entered at or shortly following their birth.

If you already show your dog, if you plan on being an exhibitor in the future, or if you simply enjoy attending dog shows, there is a book, written by me, which you will find to be an invaluable source of detailed information about all aspects of show dog competition. This book is *Successful Dog Show Exhibiting* (T.F.H. Publications, Inc.) and is available wherever the one you are reading was purchased.

Ch. Donnchada's Big Shot, a multi-Group and Specialty Best in Show winner, pictured here with handler Robert N. Peebles gaining a Group award. Owned by J. Craig Osborne and B. Brown.

**Opposite page:**
Ch. Dassin De Lux taking one of her numerous Bests in Show for Mrs. Edward Solomon, Jr., at Del-Otse-Nango K.C. in 1983. Bud Dickey handling, Anna K. Nicholas the judge.

Ch. The Most Happy Hooker of Camelot, bred by Nancy and Mary Ellen Fishler, co-owned by Nancy, Marvin, and Mary Ellen Fishler, taking Best of Opposite Sex at the Watchung Mountain Poodle Club Specialty in 1982.

## *Junior Showmanship Competition*

If there is a youngster in your family between the ages of ten and sixteen, I can suggest no better or more rewarding hobby than becoming an active participant in Junior Showmanship. This is a marvelous activity for young people. It teaches responsibility, good sportsmanship, the fun of competition where one's own skills are the deciding factor of success, proper care of a pet, and how to socialize with other young folks. Any youngster may experience the thrill of emerging from the ring a winner and the satisfaction of a good job well done.

Entry in Junior Showmanship Classes is open to any boy or girl who is at least ten years old and under seventeen years old on the day of the show. The Novice Junior Showmanship Class is open to youngsters who have not already won, at the time the entries close, three firsts in this class. Youngsters who have won three firsts in Novice may compete in the Open Junior Showmanship Class. Any junior handler who wins his third first-place award in Novice may participate in the Open Class at the same show, provided that the Open Class has at least one other junior handler entered and competing in it that day. The Novice and Open Classes may be divided into Junior and Senior Classes.

Youngsters between the ages of ten and twelve, inclusively, are eligible for the Junior division; and youngsters between thirteen and seventeen, inclusively, are eligible for the Senior division.

Any of the foregoing classes may be separated into individual classes for boys and for girls. If such a division is made, it must be so indicated on the premium list. The premium list also indicates the prize for Best Junior Handler, if such a prize is being offered at the show. Any youngster who wins a first in any of the regular classes may enter the competition for this prize, provided the youngster has been undefeated in any other Junior Showmanship Class at that show.

Junior Showmanship Classes, unlike regular conformation classes in which the quality of the dog is judged, are judged solely on the skill and ability of the junior handling the dog. Which dog is best is not the point—it is which youngster does the best job with the dog that is under consideration. Eligibility requirements for the dog being shown in Junior Showmanship, and other detailed information, can be found in *Regulations for Junior Showmanship,* available from the American Kennel Club.

A junior who has a dog that he or she can enter in both Junior Showmanship and conformation classes has twice the opportunity for success and twice the opportunity to get into the ring and work with the dog, a combination which can lead to not only awards for expert handling but also, if the dog is of sufficient quality, for making a conformation champion.

## *Pre-Show Preparations for Your Dog and You*

Preparation of the items you will need as a dog show exhibitor should not be left until the last moment. They should be planned and arranged for at least several days in advance of the show in order for you to remain calm and relaxed as the countdown starts.

The importance of the crate has already been mentioned, and we hope it is already part of your equipment. Of equal importance is the grooming table, which very likely you have also already acquired for use at home. You should take it along with you to the shows, as your dog will need last minute touches before entering the ring. Should you have not yet made this purchase, folding tables with rubber tops are made specifically for this purpose and can be purchased at most dog shows, where concession booths with marvelous assortments of "doggy" necessities are to be found, or at your pet supplier. You will also need a sturdy tack box (also available at the dog show concessions) in which to carry your grooming tools and equipment. The latter should include brushes, comb, scissors, nail clippers, whatever you use for last minute clean-up jobs, cotton swabs, first-aid equipment, and anything you are in the habit of using on the dog, including a leash or two of the type you prefer, some well-cooked and dried-out liver or any of the small packaged "dog treats" for use as bait in the ring, an atomizer in case you wish to dampen your dog's coat when you are preparing him for the ring, and so on. A large turkish towel to spread under the dog on the grooming table is also useful.

Take a large thermos or cooler of ice, the biggest one you can accommodate in your vehicle, for use by "man and beast." Take a jug of water (there are lightweight, inexpensive ones available at all sporting goods shops) and a water dish. If you plan to feed the dog at the show, or if you

Ch. Alekai Anticipation, owned by Dwaner Leona Ellis, Sturgis, South Dakota, is a daughter of Ch. Alekai Anticipation ex Ch. Alekai Brilliance.

The noted white Miniature, Ch. Round Table Conte Blanc winning Best in Show, with John Brennan handling for owners, Round Table Kennels.

and the dog will be away from home more than one day, bring food for him from home so that he will have the type to which he is accustomed.

You may or may not have an exercise pen. Personally I think one a *must*, even if you only have one dog. While the shows do provide areas for the exercise of the dogs, these are among the most likely places to have your dog come in contact with any illnesses which may be going around, and I feel that having a pen of your own for your dog's use is excellent protection. Such a pen can be used in other ways, too, such as a place other than the crate in which to put the dog to relax (that is roomier than the crate) and a place in which the dog can exercise at motels and rest areas. These, too, are available at the show concession stands and come in a variety of heights and sizes. A set of "pooper scoopers" should also be part of your equipment, along with a package of plastic bags for cleaning up after your dog.

Bring along folding chairs for the members of your party, unless all of you are fond of standing, as these are almost never provided anymore by the clubs. Have your name stamped on the chairs so that there will be no doubt as to whom the chairs belong. Bring whatever you and your family enjoy for drinks or snacks in a picnic basket or cooler, as show food, in general, is expensive and usually not great. You should always have a pair of boots, a raincoat, and a rain hat with

Ch. Deryabar Pirate going Best of Breed at Poodle Club of Massachusetts Specialty under Mrs. Jesse Mason. Wendell J. Sammet handling for Mr. and Mrs. Royal E. Peterson, II, Deryabar Kennels, Greenwich, Conn.

you (they should remain permanently in your vehicle if you plan to attend shows regularly), as well as a sweater, a warm coat, and a change of shoes. A smock or big cover-up apron will assure that you remain tidy as you prepare the dog for the ring. Your overnight case should include a small sewing kit for emergency repairs, bandaids, headache and indigestion remedies, and any personal products or medications you normally use.

In your car you should always carry maps of the area where you are headed and an assortment of motel directories. Generally speaking, we have found Holiday Inns to be the nicest about taking dogs. Ramadas and Howard Johnsons generally do so cheerfully (with a few exceptions). Best Western generally frowns on pets (not always, but often enough to make it necessary to find out which do). Some of the smaller chains welcome pets. The majority of privately owned motels do not.

Have everything prepared the night before the show to expedite your departure. Be sure that the dog's identification and your judging program and other show information are in your purse or briefcase. If you are taking sandwiches, have them ready. Anything that goes into the car the night before the show will be one thing less to remember in the morning. Decide upon what you will wear and have it out and ready. If there is any question in your mind about what to wear, try on the possibilities before the day of the show; don't risk feeling you may want to change when you see yourself dressed a few moments prior to departure time!

In planning your outfit, make it something simple that will not detract from your dog. Remember that a dark dog silhouettes attractively against a light background and vice-versa. Sport clothes always seem to look best at dog shows, preferably conservative in type and not overly "loud" as you do not want to detract from your dog, who should be the focus of interest at this point. What you wear on your feet is important. Many types of flooring can be hazardously slippery, as can wet grass. Make it a habit to wear rubber soles and low or flat heels in the ring for your own safety, especially if you are showing a dog that likes to move out smartly.

Your final step in pre-show preparation is to leave yourself plenty of time to reach the show that morning. Traffic can get amazingly heavy as one nears the immediate area of the show, finding a parking place can be difficult, and other delays may occur. You'll be in better humor to enjoy the day if your trip to the show is not fraught with panic over fear of not arriving in time!

Ch. Dassin's Marmalade of Valcopy, owned by Maureen Mattox and Sandra Manicote and handled by Robert N. Peebles, winning here under judge Lois McManus.

Ch. Rimskittle Riot taking Best in Show at Whidbey Island. Tim brazier handling for owner, Mrs. Margaret Durney, Malibu, California.

Ch. Valcopy Bogart, noted Variety and Group winner, by Ch. McKernan Redford of Valcopy ex Wavir Whipped Cream, was bred by Dana L. Plonkey, Alderwood Manor, Washington.

## *Enjoying the Dog Show*

From the moment of your arrival at the show until after your dog has been judged, keep foremost in your mind the fact that he is your reason for being there and that he should therefore be the center of your attention. Arrive early enough to have time for those last-minute touches that can make such a great difference when he enters the ring. Be sure that he has ample time to exercise and that he attends to personal matters. A dog arriving in the ring and immediately using it as an exercise pen hardly makes a favorable impression on the judge.

When you reach ringside, ask the steward for your arm-card and anchor it firmly into place on your arm. Make sure that you are where you should be when your class is called. The fact that you have picked up your arm-card does not guarantee, as some seem to think, that the judge will wait for you. The judge has a full schedule which he wishes to complete on time. Even though you may be nervous, assume an air of calm self-confidence. Remember that this is a hobby to be enjoyed, so approach it in that state of mind. The dog will do better, too, as he will be quick to reflect your attitude.

Always show your dog with an air of pride. If you make mistakes in presenting him, don't worry about it. Next time you will do better. Do not permit the presence of more experienced exhibitors to intimidate you. After all, they, too, once were newcomers.

The judging routine usually starts when the judge asks that the dogs be gaited in a circle around the ring. During this period the judge is watching each dog as it moves, noting style, topline, reach and drive, head and tail carriage, and general balance. Keep your mind and your eye on your dog, moving him at his most becoming gait and keeping your place in line without coming too close to the exhibitor ahead of you. Always keep your dog on the inside of the circle, between yourself and the judge, so that the judge's view of the dog is unobstructed.

Calmly pose the dog when requested to set up for examination whether on the ground or on a table. If you are at the head of the line and many dogs are in the class, go all the way to the end of the ring before starting to stack the dog, leaving sufficient space for those behind you to line theirs up as well as requested by the judge. If you are not at the head of the line but between other exhibitors, leave sufficient space ahead of your dog for the judge to examine him. The dogs should be spaced so that the judge is able to move among them to see them from all angles. In practicing to "set up" or "stack" your dog for the judge's examination, bear in mind the importance of doing so

Mrs. S.J. Fishman's Ch. Rondelay Honey Bun winning Best in Show under Col. Edward McQuown.

quickly and with dexterity. The judge has a schedule to meet and only a few moments in which to evaluate each dog. You will immeasurably help yours to make a favorable impression if you are able to "get it all together" in a minimum amount of time. Practice at home before a mirror can be a great help toward bringing this about, facing the dog so that you see him from the same side that the judge will and working to make him look right in the shortest length of time.

Listen carefully as the judge describes the manner in which the dog is to be gaited, whether it is straight down and straight back; down the ring, across, and back; or in a triangle. The latter has become the most popular pattern with the majority of judges. "In a triangle" means the dog should move down the outer side of the ring to the first corner, across that end of the ring to the second corner, and then back to the judge from the second corner, using the center of the ring in a diagonal line. Please learn to do this pattern without breaking at each corner to twirl the dog around you, a senseless maneuver we sometimes have noted. Judges like to see the dog in an uninterrupted triangle, as they are thus able to get a better idea of the dog's gait.

It is impossible to overemphasize that the gait at which you move your dog is tremendously important, and considerable study and thought should be given to the matter. At home, have someone move the dog for you at different speeds so that you can tell which shows him off to best advantage. The most becoming action almost invariably is seen at a moderate gait, head up and topline holding. Do not gallop your dog around the ring or hurry him into a speed atypical of his breed. Nothing being rushed appears at its best; give your dog a chance to move along at his (and the breed's) natural gait. For a dog's action to be judged accurately, that dog should move with strength and power but not excessive speed, holding a straight line as he goes to and from the judge.

As you bring the dog back to the judge, stop him a few feet away and be sure that he is standing in a becoming position. Bait him to show the judge an alert expression, using whatever tasty morsel he has been trained to expect for this purpose or, if that works better for you, use a small squeak-toy in your hand. A reminder, please, to those using liver or treats. Take them with you when you leave the ring. Do not just drop them on the ground where they will be found by another dog.

When the awards have been made, accept yours graciously, no matter how you actually may feel about it. What's done is done, and arguing with a judge or stomping out of the ring is useless and a reflection on your sportsmanship. Be courteous, congratulate the winner if your dog was defeated, and try not to show your disappointment. By the same token, please be a gracious winner; this, surprisingly, sometimes seems to be still more difficult.

Phillippe of Bryn Mawr, C.D., owned by Miss Geraldine Harrison, with professional handler Annabelle Feldman. This apricot Standard Poodle, at Fort Lauderdale Dog Club, on January 13th 1961, scored 198½ under Mr. C.W. Bliss in Novice Class, scored High in Trial, and in conformation won Best of Variety that day under J.J. Duncan. Two days later, at Greater Miami, scored 199½ under Mrs. Pearsall, again High in Trial, and was Reserve Winners in the conformation judging.

# Chapter 14

# *Your Dog and Obedience*

For its own protection and safety, every dog should be taught, at the very least, to recognize and obey the commands "Come," "Heel," "Down," "Sit," and "Stay." Doing so at some time might save the dog's life and in less extreme circumstances will certainly make him a better behaved, more pleasant member of society. If you are patient and enjoy working with your dog, study some of the excellent books available on the subject of obedience and then teach your canine friend these basic manners. If you need the stimulus of working with a group, find out where obedience training classes are held (usually your veterinarian, your dog's breeder, or a dog-owning friend can tell you) and you and your dog can join up. Alternatively, you could let someone else do the training by sending the dog to class, but this is not very rewarding because you lose the opportunity of working with your dog and the pleasure of the rapport thus established.

If you are going to do it yourself, there are some basic rules which you should follow. You must remain calm and confident in attitude. Never lose your temper and frighten or punish your dog unjustly. Be quick and lavish with praise each time a command is correctly followed. Make it fun for the dog and he will be eager to please you by responding correctly. Repetition is the keynote, but it should not be continued without recess to the point of tedium. Limit the training sessions to ten- or fifteen-minute periods at a time.

Teddy and Joe Longo are the owners of these Poodle stars of the obedience world, relaxing to enjoy a holiday party. These well-behaved Poodles must be very eager to start on the Nylabone® on their plates.

**Opposite page:**
Highest Scoring in Trial, April 12th 1968, Andrews Nimbus of Tenali, owned by Irene V. Andrews, with a score of 198 at the Obedience Training Club of Anchorage, Alaska.

## Obedience Competition

Formal obedience training can be followed, and very frequently is, by entering the dog in obedience competition to work toward an obedience degree, or several of them, depending on the dog's aptitude and your own enjoyment. Obedience trials are held in conjunction with the majority of all-breed conformation dog shows, with Specialty shows, and frequently as separate Specialty events. If you are working alone with your dog, a list of trial dates might be obtained from your dog's veterinarian, your dog breeder, or a dog-owning friend; the A.K.C. *Gazette* lists shows and trials to be scheduled in the coming months; and if you are a member of a training class, you will find the information readily available.

The goals for which one works in the formal A.K.C. Member or Licensed Trials are the following titles: Companion Dog (C.D.), Companion Dog Excellent (C.D.X.), and Utility Dog (U.D.). These degrees are earned by receiving three "legs," or qualifying scores, at each level of competition. The degrees must be earned in order, with one completed prior to starting work on the next. For example, a dog must have earned C.D. prior to starting work on C.D.X.; then C.D.X. must be completed before U.D. work begins. The ultimate title attainable in obedience work is Obedience Trial Champion (O.T.Ch.).

When you see the letters "C.D." following a dog's name, you will know that this dog has satisfactorily completed the following exercises: heel on leash, heel free, stand for examination, recall, long sit and long stay. "C.D.X." means that tests have been passed on all of those just mentioned plus heel free, drop on recall, retrieve over high jump, broad jump, long sit, and long down. "U.D." indicates that the dog has additionally passed tests in scent discrimination (leather article), scent discrimination (metal article), signal exercises, directed retrieve, directed jumping, and group stand for examination. The letters "O.T.Ch." are the abbreviation for the only obedience title which precedes rather than follows a dog's name. To gain an obedience trial championship, a dog who already holds a Utility Dog degree must win a total of one hundred points and must win three firsts, under three different judges, in Utility and Open B Classes.

There is also a Tracking Dog title (T.D.) which can be earned at tracking trials. In order to pass the tracking tests the dog must follow the trail of a stranger along a path on which the trail was laid between thirty minutes and two hours previously. Along this track there must be more than two right-angle turns, at least two of which are well out

Paragon's Tall, Dark 'n Handsome, C.D., bred by J. Craig and Mrs. R.M. Osborne, owned by J. Craig Osborne, is the most beloved house pet at Ted-El, a favorite with all whom he has met. To quote Mr. Osborne, "A real *Poodle* in every sense of the word."

Ch. Vulcan Psyche of Gayshaws was the Crufts Utility Group winner in 1969. Owned by Miss A.C. Coppage, Taunton, Somerset, England. Wish Upon A Star is the granddaughter of Psyche, and her great granddaughter is Ch. Vulcan Champagne Ovature who won bitch Challenge Certificate, Crufts 1984.

Littlebit Fille Dorie, owned and handled by Mrs. M.H. Martin, Corpus Christi, Texas, winning High in Trial with a score of 199 under judge H.B. Richards, in May 1968.

in the open where no fences or other boundaries exist for the guidance of the dog or the handler. The dog wears a harness and is connected to the handler by a lead twenty to forty feet in length. Inconspicuously dropped at the end of the track is an article to be retrieved, usually a glove or wallet, which the dog is expected to locate and the handler to pick up. The letters "T.D.X." are the abbreviation for Tracking Dog Excellent, a more difficult version of the Tracking Dog test with a longer track and more turns to be worked through.

232

# An Australian Obedience Star

## by Judith McMahon

Poodles are popular obedience dogs in Australia. The good ones make their presence felt in competition; in fact the first official Agility Test held in Australia (in November of 1983) was won by a Miniature Poodle. But the most successful obedience Poodle of recent years in this country is a Standard bitch, Hollyfield Fleur, U.D., owned and handled by Anne Brogan of Sydney.

Anne's involvement in obedience trialling had spanned many years and several breeds before she acquired her first Standard Poodle in 1975. This was a brown bitch puppy, Rouvain Regal Sophia, the progeny of Australian Champion Springett Madrigal (an English import of mostly Bibelots breeding) and Australian Champion Hauteur Wild Thyme who was a Sydney Royal Show challenge winner. Anne trialled Sophia through to her C.D.X. title and, in 1978, bred a litter from her by Sayantsi Black Prince, a young dog sired by another Sydney Royal challenge winner, Australian Champion Marsail Gay Hi Stepper.

Anne had bred this litter with a view to keeping a dog puppy. However, from out of the tangle of seven typically lively babies, it was a bitch who kept drawing the breeder's eye. This little bitch learned quickly that whenever a visitor called, one of her littermates would disappear from the house, so she would hide in the laundry whenever strangers arrived.

Intrigued by this early display of savvy, Anne conspired with the pup by closing the laundry door after her. In a matter of weeks, the littermates had gone to various new homes and only the little girl remained. At this stage, she attached herself to Anne, following her quietly about the house, sitting unobtrusively within view of her owner, and simply staring at her "fellow human." Anne felt a strong psychic link between them and soon discovered the pup to be a rapid learner and an intuitive worker.

Registered as Hollyfield Fleur, but known to all as "Bindi," the youngster and her owner started working towards competition. At ten months of age "Bindi" qualified for her C.D. title in three straight trials. Her C.D.X. was achieved shortly afterwards when she was only fifteen months of age. Then began a campaign at Open level to win the best awards available to obedience dogs on the eastern side of the Australian continent.

Hollyfield Fleur, C.D.X., U.D., Australia's fantastic obedience Poodle "star."

En route to her U.D. title, which was achieved in four trials, "Bindi" took the following awards: winner of Highest Point Score in Trial, Poodle Club of NSW Championship Show and Trial specialties, six times; Gold Medallion Winner (first placing) at two Sydney Spring Fair Dog Shows; first place winner in Open Bitch Class at two Sydney Royal Shows; first place winner in Open Bitch Class at the National Obedience Titles; Winner of Winners at Melbourne Royal Show; Winner of Winners at Canberra Royal Shows (once from Utility Class), three times; Obedience Club Champion of Metropolitan Midweek Dog Training Club for four years in succession; and the prestigious Jack Goldstein Memorial Trophy, an annual award given to the highest scoring competitor over seven specified obedience trials, twice.

It is interesting to note "Bindi's" figures. Over the past twelve months she has competed in 30 Open and Utility Classes for 25 first placings, four seconds and one third. Her average score has been 195 points out of the possible 200; her highest score stands at 199 points.

Despite the consistency of her winning, "Bindi" is no "robot." She is a delight to watch in her work, enjoying that rare combination of irrepressible *joie de vivre* and extraordinary concentration with which only very special obedience dogs seem to be blessed.

As a break from obedience trialling, Anne also trained "Bindi" for tracking and gundog work. Tracking certificates are required for her Australian obedience champion title, though the work holds little fascination for Anne. Gundog work, on the other hand, is something both "Bindi" and her trainer relish. With the blessing of one Sydney club, "Bindi" was entered at a Gundog Obedience Trial and retrieved her bird in splendid style. As a representative of the Non-Sporting Group, however, she is ineligible to compete officially, a state of affairs which Anne finds rather disappointing. Ideally, she would like to find support and approval for a team of Poodles to participate on gundog training days, as is done in the United States.

Two of Bindi's littermates have also found success in the obedience rings. Hollyfield Sophia was trialled to her C.D.X. title by Anne's mother, and Hollyfield Don Juan came back to Anne and also achieved his C.D.X. He is currently being trained by Anne for hurdling and agility work which are fast becoming enormously popular spectator events with the Australian public.

The great Best in Show Standard bitch, Ch. Dassin Rita La Rose, owned by Mrs. Edward Solomon, handled to a highly successful ring career by Freeman Dickey.

# Chapter 15

# *Breeding Your Poodle*

## *The Poodle Brood Bitch*

We have in an earlier chapter discussed selection of a bitch you plan to use for breeding. In making this important purchase, you will be choosing a bitch who you hope will become the foundation of your kennel. Thus she must be of the finest producing bloodlines, excellent in temperament, of good type, and free of major faults or unsoundness. If you are offered a "bargain" brood bitch, be wary, as for this purchase you should not settle for less than the best and the price will be in accordance with the quality.

Conscientious breeders feel quite strongly that the only possible reason for producing puppies is the ambition to improve and uphold quality and temperament within the breed—definitely *not* because one hopes to make a quick cash profit on a mediocre litter, which never seems to work out that way in the long run and which accomplishes little beyond perhaps adding to the nation's heartbreaking number of unwanted canines. The only reason ever for breeding a litter is, with conscientious people, a desire to improve the quality of dogs in their own kennel or, as pet owners, because they wish to add to the number of dogs they themselves own with a puppy or two from their present favorites. In either case breeding should not take place unless one has definitely prospective owners for as many puppies as the litter may contain, lest you find yourself with several fast-growing young dogs and no homes in which to place them.

Bitches should not be mated earlier than their second season, by which time they should be from fifteen to eighteen months old. Many breeders prefer to wait and first finish the championships of their show bitches before breeding them, as pregnancy can be a disaster to a show coat and getting the bitch back in shape again takes time. When you have decided what will be the proper time, start watching at least several months ahead for what you feel would be the perfect mate to best complement your bitch's quality and bloodlines. Subscribe to the magazines which feature your breed exclusively and to some which cover all breeds in order to familiarize yourself with outstanding stud dogs in areas other than your own for there is no necessity nowadays to limit your choice to a nearby dog unless you truly like him and feel that he is the most suitable. It is quite usual to ship a bitch to a stud dog a distance away, and this generally works out with no ill effects. The important thing is that you need a stud dog strong in those features where your bitch is weak or lacking and of bloodlines compatible to hers. Compare the background of both your bitch and the stud dog under consideration, paying particular attention to the quality of the puppies from bitches with backgrounds similar to your bitch's. If the puppies have been of the type and quality you admire, then this dog would seem a sensible choice for yours, too.

Stud fees may be a few hundred dollars, sometimes even more under special situations for a particularly successful sire. It is money well spent, however. Do *not* ever breed to a dog because he is less expensive than the others unless you honestly believe that he can sire the kind of puppies who will be a credit to your kennel and your breed.

Contacting the owners of the stud dogs you find interesting will bring you pedigrees and pictures which you can then study in relation to your bitch's pedigree and conformation. Discuss your plans with other breeders who are knowledgeable (including the one who bred your own bitch). You may not always receive an entirely unbiased opinion (particularly if the person giving it also has an available stud dog), but one learns by discussion so listen to what they say, consider their opinions, and then you may be better qualified to form your own opinion.

As soon as you have made a choice, phone the owner of the stud dog you wish to use to find out if this will be agreeable. You will be asked about the bitch's health, soundness, temperament, and freedom from serious faults. A copy of her pedigree may be requested, as might a picture of her. A discussion of her background over the telephone may be sufficient to assure the stud's owner that she is suitable for the stud dog and of type, breeding, and quality herself to produce puppies of the quality for which the dog is noted. The owner of a top-quality stud is

Ch. Alekai Phaedra, owned by Dorothy Matzner and handled by Wendell Sammet, is a litter sister to Ch. Alekai Zephyr. Dam of five American Champions, one Canadian Champion, and one Nordic International C.A.C.I.B. winner.

often extremely selective in the bitches permitted to be bred to his dog, in an effort to keep the standard of his puppies high. The owner of a stud dog may require that the bitch be tested for brucellosis, which should be attended to not more than a month previous to the breeding.

Check out which airport will be most convenient for the person meeting and returning the bitch if she is to be shipped and also what airlines use that airport. You will find that the airlines are also apt to have special requirements concerning acceptance of animals for shipping. These include weather limitations and types of crates which are acceptable. The weather limits have to do with extreme heat and extreme cold at the point of destination, as some airlines will not fly dogs into

Ch. Dhubne Darth
Vader and kids.
Caroll Ann Irwin,
owner, North
Hollywood,
California.

temperatures above or below certain levels, fearing for their safety. The crate problem is a simple one, since if your own crate is not suitable, most of the airlines have specially designed crates available for purchase at a fair and moderate price. It is a good plan to purchase one of these if you intend to be shipping dogs with any sort of frequency. They are made of fiberglass and are the safest type to use for shipping.

Normally you must notify the airline several days in advance to make a reservation, as they are able to accommodate only a certain number of dogs on each flight. Plan on shipping the bitch on about her eighth or ninth day of season, but be careful to avoid shipping her on a weekend, when schedules often vary and freight offices are apt to be closed. Whenever you can, ship your bitch on a direct flight. Changing planes always carries a certain amount of risk of a dog being overlooked or wrongly routed at the middle stop, so avoid this danger if at all possible. The bitch must be accompanied by a health certificate which you must obtain from your veterinarian before taking her to the airport. Usually it will be necessary to have the bitch at the airport about two hours prior to flight time. Before finalizing arrangements, find out from the stud's owner at what time of day it will be most convenient to have the bitch picked up promptly upon arrival.

It is simpler if you can plan to bring the bitch to the stud dog. Some people feel that the trauma of the flight may cause the bitch to not conceive; and, of course, undeniably there is a slight risk in shipping which can be avoided if you are able to drive the bitch to her destination. Be sure to leave yourself sufficient time to assure your arrival at the right time for her for breeding (normally the tenth to fourteenth day following the first signs of color); and remember that if you want the bitch bred twice, you should allow a day to elapse between the two matings. Do not expect the stud's owner to house you while you are there. Locate a nearby motel that takes dogs and make that your headquarters.

Just prior to the time your bitch is due in season, you should take her to visit your veterinarian. She should be checked for worms and should receive all the booster shots for which she is due plus one for parvo virus, unless she has had the latter shot fairly recently. The brucellosis test can also be done then, and the health certificate can be obtained for shipping if she is to travel by air. Should the bitch be at all overweight, now is the time to get the surplus off. She should be in good condition, neither underweight nor overweight, at the time of breeding.

The moment you notice the swelling of the vulva, for which you should be checking daily as the time for her season approaches, and

Ch. Story Tale Full of Pride (son of Ch. Dassin Debauchery), bred by Mrs. J. Bachner, owned by William H. Williams, Jr., handled by Robert N. Peebles.

Four generations of Miniatures, representing some of England's finest bloodlines: Ch. Berita's Ronlyn Rockefella, Top Producer, *on the left;* his son, Ch. Bentwater Beritas Shiloh, Top Producer, *second from left;* Shiloh's son, Ch. Bentwater Aztec, Top Producer, *next;* and Aztec's son, Champion Helsonae Sunday Special *on the right.* Photo courtesy of Dassin Farm, Freeman Dickey and Joseph Vergnetti.

the appearance of color, immediately contact the stud's owner and settle on the day for shipping or make the appointment for your arrival with the bitch for breeding. If you are shipping the bitch, the stud fee check should be mailed immediately, leaving ample time for it to have been received when the bitch arrives and the mating takes place. Be sure to call the airline making her reservation at that time, too.

Do not feed the bitch within a few hours before shipping her. Be certain that she has had a drink of water and been well exercised before closing her in the crate. Several layers of newspapers, topped with some shredded newspaper, make a good bed and can be discarded when she arrives at her destination; these can be replaced with fresh newspapers for her return home. Remember that the bitch should be brought to the airport about two hours before flight time as sometimes the airlines refuse to accept late arrivals.

If you are taking your bitch by car, be certain that you will arrive at a reasonable time of day. Do not appear late in the evening. If your arrival in town is not until late, get a good night's sleep at your motel and contact the stud's owner first thing in the morning. If possible, leave children and relatives at home, as they will only be in the way and perhaps unwelcome by the stud's owner. Most stud dog owners prefer not to have any unnecessary people on hand during the actual mating.

Ch. Yerbrier Done To Perfection with her handler Freeman Dickey who piloted her to many a hotly contested Best In Show for owner Betty Yerringer.

After the breeding has taken place, if you wish to sit and visit for awhile and the stud's owner has the time, return the bitch to her crate in your car (first ascertaining, of course, that the temperature is comfortable for her and that there is proper ventilation. She should not be permitted to urinate for at least one hour following the breeding. This is the time when you get the business part of the transaction attended to. Pay the stud fee, upon which you should receive your breeding certificate and, if you do not already have it, a copy of the stud dog's pedigree. The owner of the stud dog does not sign or furnish a litter registration application until the puppies have been born.

Upon your return home, you can settle down and plan in happy anticipation a wonderful litter of puppies. A word of caution! Remember that although she has been bred, your bitch is still an interesting target for all male dogs, so guard her carefully for the next week or until you are absolutely certain that her season has entirely ended. This would be no time to have any unfortunate incident with another dog.

Am., Can., Mex., and Int. Ch. Jodan's Orange Delight, bred and owned by Mr. and Mrs. Daniel O. Gallas, is pictured here taking the *first Toy Group ever won* by the now famed professional handler Robert N. Peebles.

Ch. Carlynn's Lady Imperial at Victoria K.C. in 1982. This was Winners Bitch in Miniatures at P.C.A. that year, handled by Robert N. Peebles for owner Karen Wright.

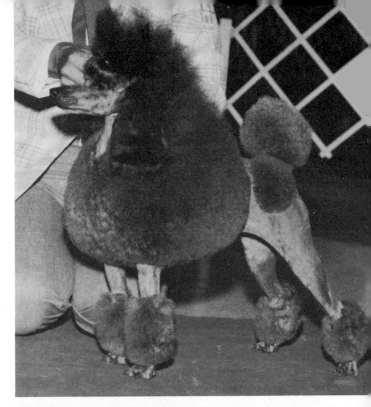

"Black and White." Ch. Dassin De Lux with F.C. Dickey and Dassin Daydream with Joseph Vergnetti. Photo courtesy of owner, Mrs. Edward Solomon, Pittsburgh, Pa. Richard Hensel judging.

BEST OF
BREED
OR VARIETY

PHOTO BY K. BOOTH

## The Poodle Stud Dog

Choosing the best stud dog to complement your bitch is often very difficult. The two principal factors to be considered should be the stud's conformation and his pedigree. Conformation is fairly obvious; you want a dog that is typical of the breed in the words of the standard of perfection. Understanding pedigrees is a bit more subtle since the pedigree lists the ancestry of the dog and involves individuals and bloodlines with which you may not be entirely familiar.

To a novice in the breed, then, the correct interpretation of a pedigree may at first be difficult to grasp. Study the pictures and text of this book and you will find many names of important bloodlines and members of the breed. Also make an effort to discuss the various dogs behind the proposed stud with some of the more experienced breeders, starting with the breeder of your own bitch. Frequently these folks will be personally familiar with many of the dogs in question, can offer opinions of them, and may have access to additional pictures which you would benefit by seeing.

It is very important that the stud's pedigree should be harmonious with that of the bitch you plan on breeding to him. Do not rush out and breed to the latest winner with no thought of whether or not he can produce true quality. By no means are all great show dogs great producers. It is the producing record of the dog in question and the dogs and bitches from which he has come which should be the basis on which you make your choice.

Breeding dogs is never a money-making operation. By the time you pay a stud fee, care for the bitch during pregnancy, whelp the litter, and rear the puppies through their early shots, worming, and so on, you will be fortunate to break even financially once the puppies have been sold. Your chances of doing this are greater if you are breeding for a show-quality litter which will bring you higher prices as the pups are sold as show prospects. Therefore, your wisest investment is to use the best dog available for your bitch regardless of the cost; then you should wind up with more valuable puppies. Remember that it is equally costly to raise mediocre puppies as top ones, and your chances of financial return are better on the latter. To breed to the most excellent, most suitable stud dog you can find is the only sensible thing to do, and it is poor economy to quibble over the amount you are paying in stud fee.

It will be your decision which course you decide to follow when you breed your bitch, as there are three options: linebreeding, inbreeding,

The Top Producing Standard Poodle *of all time,* Ch. Dassin Debauchery, sire of 85 or more champions, was bred by Freeman Dickey and Joan E. Sonilko. Here winning Best Standard Poodle at the Poodle Club of America Specialty in 1974, handled by Robert N. Peebles under judge Mrs. Jean Lyle. Owned by Joyce and Stuart Bachner, Story Tale Poodles.

and outcrossing. Each of these methods has its supporters and its detractors! Linebreeding is breeding a bitch to a dog belonging originally to the same canine family, being descended from the same ancestors, such as half-brother to half-sister, grandsire to grand-daughters, niece to uncle (and vice-versa) or cousin to cousin. Inbreeding is breeding father to daughter, mother to son, or full brother to sister. Outcross breeding is breeding a dog and a bitch with no or only a few mutual ancestors.

Linebreeding is probably the safest course, and the one most likely to bring results, for the novice breeder. The more sophisticated inbreeding should be left to the experienced, long-time breeders who thoroughly know and understand the risks and the possibilities involved with a particular line. It is usually done in an effort to intensify some ideal feature in that strain. Outcrossing is the reverse of inbreeding, an effort to introduce improvement in a specific feature needing correction, such as a shorter back, better movement, more correct head or coat, and so on.

It is the serious breeder's ambition to develop a strain or bloodline of their own, one strong in qualities for which their dogs will become distinguished. However, it must be realized that this will involve time, patience, and at least several generations before the achievement can be claimed. The safest way to embark on this plan, as we have mentioned, is by the selection and breeding of one or two bitches, the best you can buy and from top-producing kennels. In the beginning you do *not* really have to own a stud dog. In the long run it is less expensive and sounder judgment to pay a stud fee when you are ready to breed a bitch than to purchase a stud dog and feed him all year; a stud dog does not win any popularity contests with owners of bitches to be bred until he becomes a champion, has been successfully Specialed for awhile, and has been at least moderately advertised, all of which adds up to a quite healthy expenditure.

The wisest course for the inexperienced breeder just starting out in dogs is as I have outlined above. Keep the best bitch puppy from the first several litters. After that you may wish to consider keeping your own stud dog if there has been a particularly handsome male in one of your litters that you feel has great potential or if you know where there is one available that you are interested in, with the feeling that he would work in nicely with the breeding program on which you have embarked. By this time, with several litters already born, your eye should have developed to a point enabling you to make a wise choice, either from one of your own litters or from among dogs you have seen that appear suitable.

The greatest care should be taken in the selection of your own stud dog. He must be of true type and highest quality as he may be responsible for siring many puppies each year, and he should come from a line of excellent dogs on both sides of his pedigree which themselves are, and which are descended from, successful producers. This dog should have no glaring faults in conformation; he should be of such quality that he can hold his own in keenest competition within his breed. He should be in good health, be virile and be a keen stud dog, a proven sire able to transmit his correct qualities to his puppies. Need I say that such a dog will be enormously expensive unless you have the good fortune to produce him in one of your own litters? To buy and use a lesser stud dog, however, is downgrading your breeding program unnecessarily since there are so many dogs fitting the description of a fine stud whose services can be used on payment of a stud fee.

You should *never* breed to an unsound dog or one with any serious standard or disqualifying faults. Not all champions by any means pass along their best features; and by the same token, occasionally you will find a great one who can pass along his best features but never gained his championship title due to some unusual circumstances. The information you need about a stud dog is what type of puppies he has produced and with what bloodlines and whether or not he possesses the bloodlines and attributes considered characteristic of the best in your breed.

If you go out to buy a stud dog, obviously he will not be a puppy but rather a fully mature and proven male with as many of the best attributes as possible. True, he will be an expensive investment, but if you choose and make his selection with care and forethought, he may well prove to be one of the best investments you have ever made.

Of course, the most exciting of all is when a young male you have decided to keep from one of your litters due to his tremendous show potential turns out to be a stud dog such as we have described. In this case he should be managed with care, for he is a valuable property that can contribute inestimably to his breed as a whole and to your own kennel specifically.

Do not permit your stud dog to be used until he is about a year old, and even then he should be bred to a mature, proven matron accustomed to breeding who will make his first experience pleasant and easy. A young dog can be put off forever by a maiden bitch who fights and resists his advances. Never allow this to happen. Always start a

Ch. Dassin Debussy, noted show dog and producer, with Joseph Vergnetti taking a Group in 1978 and Anna Katherine Nicholas judging.

stud dog out with a bitch who is mature, has been bred previously, and is of even temperament. The first breeding should be performed in quiet surroundings with only you and one other person to hold the bitch. Do not make it a circus, as the experience will determine the dog's outlook about future stud work. If he does not enjoy the first experience or associates it with any unpleasantness, you may well have a problem in the future.

Your young stud must permit help with the breeding, as later there will be bitches who will not be cooperative. If right from the beginning you are there helping him and praising him whether or not your assistance is actually needed, he will expect and accept this as a matter of course when a difficult bitch comes along.

Carawyn Luke Skywalker, Grand Champion Poodle Club of Southern California, bred by Elizabeth Campbell and Irene Hauner. Owned by Jack Heidinger. This is a son of Ch. Dhubne Darth Vader, Carroll Ann Irwin's famous dog.

Ch. Eaton Ensign, multiple Best in Show winner, by Ch. Allyah Desperado ex Ch. Eaton Busting with Joy. Owner-handler, Dana Plonkey, Valcopy Kennels, Alderwood Manor, Washington. This dog is a litter brother to Ch. Eaton Affirmed.

Things to have handy before introducing your dog and the bitch are K-Y jelly (the only lubricant which should be used) and a length of gauze with which to muzzle the bitch should it be necessary to keep her from biting you or the dog. Some bitches put up a fight; others are calm. It is best to be prepared.

At the time of the breeding the stud fee comes due, and it is expected that it will be paid promptly. Normally a return service is offered in case the bitch misses or fails to produce one live puppy. Conditions of the service are what the stud dog's owner makes them, and there are no standard rules covering this. The stud fee is paid for the act, not the result. If the bitch fails to conceive, it is customary for the owner to offer a free return service; but this is a courtesy and not to be considered a right, particularly in the case of a proven stud who is siring consistently and whose fault the failure obviously is *not*. Stud dog owners are always anxious to see their clients get good value and to have in the ring winning young stock by their dog; therefore, very few refuse to mate the second time. It is wise, however, for both parties to have the terms of the transaction clearly understood at the time of the breeding.

If the return service has been provided and the bitch has missed a second time, that is considered to be the end of the matter and the owner would be expected to pay a further fee if it is felt that the bitch should be given a third chance with the stud dog. The management of a stud dog and his visiting bitches is quite a task, and a stud fee has usually been well earned when one service has been achieved, let alone by repeated visits from the same bitch.

The accepted litter is one live puppy. It is wise to have printed a breeding certificate which the owner of the stud dog and the owner of the bitch both sign. This should list in detail the conditions of the breeding as well as the dates of the mating.

Upon occasion, arrangements other than a stud fee in cash are made for a breeding, such as the owner of the stud taking a pick-of-the-litter puppy in lieu of money. This should be clearly specified on the breeding certificate along with the terms of the age at which the stud's owner will select the puppy, whether it is to be a specific sex, or whether it is to be the pick of the entire litter.

The price of a stud fee varies according to circumstances. Usually, to prove a young stud dog, his owner will allow the first breeding to be quite inexpensive. Then, once a bitch has become pregnant by him, he becomes a "proven stud" and the fee rises accordingly for bitches that follow. The sire of championship-quality puppies will bring a stud fee of at least the purchase price of one show puppy as the accepted "rule-of-thumb." Until at least one champion by your stud dog has finished, the fee will remain equal to the price of one pet puppy. When his list of champions starts to grow, so does the amount of the stud fee. For a top-producing sire of champions, the stud fee will rise accordingly.

Almost invariably it is the bitch who comes to the stud dog for the breeding. Immediately upon having selected the stud dog you wish to use, discuss the possibility with the owner of that dog. It is the stud dog owner's prerogative to refuse to breed any bitch deemed unsuitable for his dog. Stud fee and method of payment should be stated at this time, and a decision reached on whether it is to be a full cash transaction at the time of the mating or a pick-of-the-litter puppy, usually at eight weeks of age.

If the owner of the stud dog must travel to an airport to meet the bitch and ship her for the flight home, an additional charge will be made for time, tolls, and gasoline based on the stud owner's proximity to the airport. The stud fee includes board for the day on the bitch's arrival through two days for breeding, with a day in between. If it is necessary that the bitch remain longer, it is very likely that additional board will be charged at the normal per-day rate for the breed.

Be sure to advise the stud's owner as soon as you know that your bitch is in season so that the stud dog will be available. This is especially important because if he is a dog being shown, he and his owner may be unavailable owing to the dog's absence from home.

As the owner of a stud dog being offered to the public, it is essential that you have proper facilities for the care of visiting bitches. Nothing can be worse than a bitch being insecurely housed and slipping out to become lost or bred by the wrong dog. If you are taking people's valued bitches into your kennel or home, it is imperative that you provide them with comfortable, secure housing and good care while they are your responsibility.

There is no dog more valuable than the proven sire of champions, Group winners and Best in Show dogs. Once you have such an animal, guard his reputation well and do *not* permit him to be bred to just any bitch that comes along. It takes two to make the puppies; even the most dominant stud can not do it all himself, so never permit him to breed a bitch you consider unworthy. Remember that when the puppies arrive, it will be your stud dog who will be blamed for any lack of quality, while the bitch's shortcomings will be quickly and conveniently overlooked.

Ch. Kirsch Delphi Moonstone, bred by Maureen Mattox and Sandra LeVaque, is by Ch. Bar J. Macho Brand of Kirsch ex Ch. Kirsch's Tava. A Specialty winner from the puppy class, she is top producing dam of Ch. Kirsch's Rodeo of Halo (Best in Show winner), Ch. Kirsch's Topsider of Bar J, and Ch. Kirsch's Izod. Handlers, R.N. Peebles and J. Craig Osborne, Houston, Texas. Owned by Maureen Mattox and Dale LeVaque.

Ch. Dassin Rhett Butler, C.D., by Ch. Dassin Debussy ex Ch. Dassin Six Pac, is a litter brother to Ch. Dassin Rita La Rose. Carroll Ann Irwin, owner, N. Hollywood, California.

Going into the actual management of the mating is a bit superfluous here. If you have had previous experience in breeding a dog and bitch you will know how the mating is done. If you do not have such experience, you should not attempt to follow directions given in a book but should have a veterinarian, breeder friend, or handler there to help you the first few times. You do not just turn the dog and bitch loose together and await developments, as too many things can go wrong and you may altogether miss getting the bitch bred. Someone should hold the dog and the bitch (one person each) until the "tie" is made and these two people should stay with them during the entire act.

If you get a complete tie, probably only the one mating is absolutely necessary. However, especially with a maiden bitch or one that has come a long distance for this breeding, we prefer following up with a second breeding, leaving one day in between the two matings. In this way there will be little or no chance of the bitch missing.

Once the tie has been completed and the dogs release, be certain that the male's penis goes completely back within its sheath. He should be allowed a drink of water and a short walk, and then he should be put into his crate or somewhere alone where he can settle down. Do not allow him to be with other dogs for a while as they will notice the odor of the bitch on him, and particularly with other males present, he may become involved in a fight.

## Pregnancy, Whelping, and the Litter

Once the bitch has been bred and is back at home, remember to keep an ever watchful eye that no other male gets to her until at least the twenty-second day of her season has passed. Until then, it will still be possible for an unwanted breeding to take place, which at this point would be catastrophic. Remember that she actually can have two separate litters by two different dogs, so take care.

In other ways, she should be treated normally. Controlled exercise is good, and necessary for the bitch throughout her pregnancy, tapering it off to just several short walks daily, preferably on lead, as she reaches about her seventh week. As her time grows close, be careful about her jumping or playing too roughly.

The theory that a bitch should be overstuffed with food when pregnant is a poor one. A fat bitch is never an easy whelper, so the overfeeding you consider good for her may well turn out to be the exact opposite. During the first few weeks of pregnancy, your bitch should be fed her normal diet. At four to five weeks along, calcium should be added to her food. At seven weeks her food may be increased if she seems to crave more than she is getting, and a meal of canned milk (mixed with an equal amount of water) should be introduced. If she is fed just once a day, add another meal rather than overload her with too much at one time. If twice a day is her schedule, then a bit more food can be added to each feeding.

A week before the pups are due, your bitch should be introduced to her whelping box so that she will be accustomed to it and feel at home there when the puppies arrive. She should be encouraged to sleep there but permitted to come and go as she wishes. The box should be roomy enough for her to lie down and stretch out but not too large lest the pups have more room than is needed in which to roam and possibly get chilled by going too far away from their mother. Be sure that the box has a "pig rail"; this will prevent the puppies from being crushed against the sides. The room in which the box is placed, either in your home or in the kennel, should be kept at about 70 degrees Fahrenheit. In winter it may be necessary to have an infrared lamp over the whelping box, in which case be careful not to place it too low or close to the puppies.

Newspapers will become a very important commodity, so start collecting them well in advance to have a big pile handy to the whelping box. With a litter of puppies, one never seems to have papers enough, so the higher pile to start with, the better off you will be. Other necessities for whelping time are clean, soft turkish towels, scissors, and a bottle of alcohol.

You will know that her time is very near when your bitch becomes restless, wandering in and out of her box and of the room. She may refuse food, and at that point her temperature will start to drop. She will dig at and tear up the newspapers in her box, shiver, and generally look uncomfortable. Only you should be with your bitch at this time. She does not need spectators; and several people, even though they may be family members whom she knows, hanging over her may upset her to the point where she may harm the puppies. You should remain nearby, quietly watching, not fussing or hovering; speak calmly and frequently to her to instill confidence. Eventually she will settle down in her box and begin panting; contractions will follow. Soon thereafter a puppy will start to emerge, sliding out with the contractions. The mother immediately should open the sac, sever the cord with her teeth, and then clean up the puppy. She will also eat the placenta, which you should permit. Once the puppy is cleaned, it should be

Ch. Dassin Danielle, sensational Miniature bitch, taking Group First from the classes, Sara-Bay K.C. 1983. Owned by Joseph Vergnetti and Freeman Dickey, Dassin Farm, Medina, Ohio.

Bentwater Bronwyn, the grandmother of Ch. Dassin Danielle.

EST OF
POSITE

GILBERT PHOTO

placed next to the bitch unless she is showing signs of having the next one immediately. Almost at once the puppy will start looking for a nipple on which to nurse, and you should ascertain that it is able to latch on successfully.

If the puppy is a breech (*i.e.*, born feet first), you must watch carefully for it to be completely delivered as quickly as possible and the sac removed quickly so that the puppy does not drown. Sometimes even a normally positioned birth will seem extremely slow in coming. Should this occur, you might take a clean towel and, as the bitch contracts, pull the puppy out, doing so gently and with utmost care. If, once the puppy is delivered, it shows little signs of life, take a rough turkish towel and massage the puppy's chest by rubbing quite briskly back and forth. Continue this for about fifteen minutes, and be sure that the mouth is free from liquid. It may be necessary to try mouth-to-mouth breathing, which is done by pressing the puppy's jaws open and, using a finger, depressing the tongue which may be stuck to the roof of the mouth. Then place your mouth against the puppy's and blow hard down the puppy's throat. Bubbles may pop out of its nose, but keep on blowing. Rub the puppy's chest with the towel again and try artificial respiration, pressing the sides of the chest together slowly and rhythmically—in and out, in and out. Keep trying one method or the other for at least twenty minutes before giving up. You may be rewarded with a live puppy who otherwise would not have made it.

If you are successful in bringing the puppy around, do not immediately put it back with the mother as it should be kept extra warm. Put it in a cardboard box on an electric heating pad or, if it is the time of year when your heat is running, near a radiator or near the fireplace or stove. As soon as the rest of the litter has been born it then can join the others.

An hour or more may elapse between puppies, which is fine so long as the bitch seems comfortable and is neither straining nor contracting. She should not be permitted to remain unassisted for more than an hour if she does continue to contract. This is when you should get her to your veterinarian, whom you should already have alerted to the possibility of a problem existing. He should examine her and perhaps give her a shot of pituitrin. In some cases the veterinarian may find that a Caesarean section is necessary due to a puppy being lodged in a manner making normal delivery impossible. Sometimes this is caused by an abnormally large puppy, or it may just be that the puppy is simply turned in the wrong position. If the bitch does require a

Ch. Dassin Debussy, Best of Variety. Ch. Dassin Busby Berkley, Best of Winners. Ch. Dassin Dancing Daffodil, Best of Opposite Sex. Three splendid Poodles from Dassin Farm, Joseph Vergnetti and Freeman Dickey, Medina, Ohio.

Caesarean section, the puppies already born must be kept warm in their cardboard box with a heating pad under the box.

Once the section is done, get the bitch and the puppies home. Do not attempt to put the puppies in with the bitch until she has regained consciousness as she may unknowingly hurt them. But do get them back to her as soon as possible for them to start nursing.

Should the mother lack milk at this time, the puppies must be fed by hand, kept very warm, and held onto the mother's teats several times a day in order to stimulate and encourage the secretion of milk, which should start shortly.

Ch. Mera's Bonux, C.D., by Carillon Loustic ex Ch. Mera's Confusion, C.D., born September 1963. Mera and Jack Monat, owners, Cincinnati, Ohio.

Assuming that there has been no problem and that the bitch has whelped naturally, you should insist that she go out to exercise, staying just long enough to make herself comfortable. She can be offered a bowl of milk and a biscuit, but then she should settle down with her family. Freshen the whelping box for her with fresh newspapers while she is taking this respite so that she and the puppies will have a clean bed.

Unless some problem arises, there is little you must do about the puppies until they become three to four weeks old. Keep the box clean and supplied with fresh newspapers the first few days, but then turkish towels should be tacked down to the bottom of the box so that the puppies will have traction as they move about.

If the bitch has difficulties with her milk supply, or if you should be so unfortunate as to lose her, then you must be prepared to either hand-feed or tube-feed the puppies if they are to survive. We personally prefer tube-feeding as it is so much faster and easier. If the bitch is available, it is best that she continues to clean and care for the puppies in the normal manner excepting for the food supplements you will provide. If it is impossible for her to do this, then after every feeding you must gently rub each puppy's abdomen with wet cotton to make it urinate, and the rectum should be gently rubbed to open the bowels.

Newborn puppies must be fed every three to four hours around the clock. The puppies must be kept warm during this time. Have your veterinarian teach you how to tube-feed. You will find that it is really quite simple.

Ch. Daikar Prince, bred and owned by Miss Betsy Rhine, Hillsboro, North Carolina was winner of the 1950's.

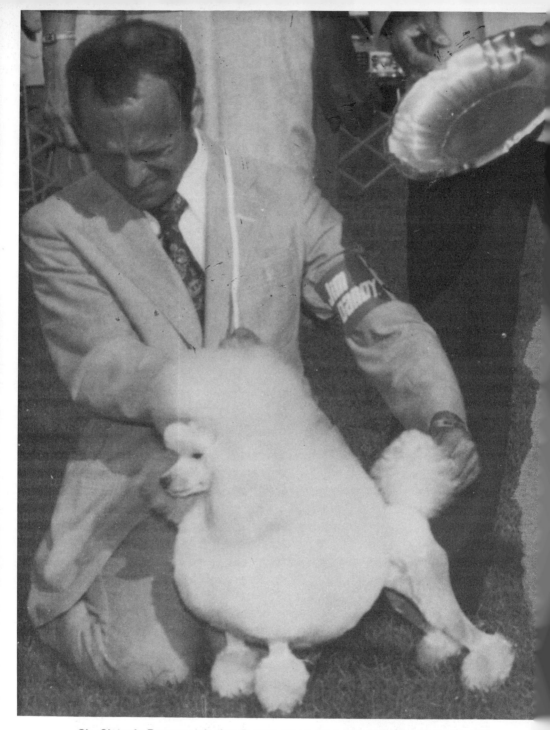

Ch. Slaton's Roxanne winning Best in Show from Mrs. Winifred Heckman. Roxanne won many Groups and Best in Show honors during her show career for owners Ross and Peggy Slaton. F.C. Dickey handling.

266

Ch. Merriwood Silver Sequin, by Ch. Bayou Breeze Silver Drop Kid ex Ch. Bayou Breeze Merriwood Flair, at Houston K.C. in 1982. Owned by Mrs. C.B. Bean.

Doral's Viking The Magician, by Ch. Midcrest Touch of Magic ex Doral's Merry Snowflake (granddaughter of Square Dancer) winning at Santa Barbara for Mrs. Dorothy S. Kenck, handled by Robert N. Peebles.

Ch. Davaroc Deja Vu winning Best Standard Poodle at Sara-Bay 1983. Owned by Mrs. Edward Solomon and Dr. and Mrs. Samuel Peacock. Freeman Dickey handling, Dassin Farm, Medina, Ohio.

After a normal whelping, the bitch will require additional food to enable her to produce sufficient milk. In addition to being fed twice daily, she should be given some canned milk several times each day.

When the puppies are two weeks old, their nails should be clipped, as they are needle sharp at this age and can hurt or damage the mother's teats and stomach as the pups hold on to nurse.

Between three and four weeks of age, the puppies should begin to be weaned. Scraped beef (prepared by scraping it off slices of beef with a spoon so that none of the gristle is included) may be offered in very small quantities a couple of times daily for the first few days. Then by the third day you can mix puppy chow with warm water as directed on the package, offering it four times daily. By now the mother should be kept away from the puppies and out of the box for several hours at a time so that when they have reached five weeks of age she is left in with them only overnight. By the time the puppies are six weeks old, they should be entirely weaned and receiving only occasional visits from their mother.

Most veterinarians recommend a temporary DHL (distemper, hepatitis, leptospirosis) shot when the puppies are six weeks of age. This remains effective for about two weeks. Then at eight weeks of age, the puppies should receive the series of permanent shots for DHL protection. It is also a good idea to discuss with your vet the advisability of having your puppies inoculated against the dreaded parvovirus at the same time. Each time the pups go to the vet for shots, you should bring stool samples so that they can be examined for worms. Worms go through various stages of development and may be present in a stool sample even though the sample does not test positive in every checkup. So do not neglect to keep careful watch on this.

The puppies should be fed four times daily until they are three months old. Then you can cut back to three feedings daily. By the time the puppies are six months of age, two meals daily are sufficient. Some people feed their dogs twice daily throughout their lifetime; others go to one meal daily when the puppy becomes one year of age.

The ideal age for puppies to go to their new homes is between eight and twelve weeks, although some puppies successfully adjust to a new home when they are six weeks old. Be sure that they go to their new owners accompanied by a description of the diet you've been feeding them and a schedule of the shots they have already received and those they still need. These should be included with the registration application and a copy of the pedigree.

Ch. Montmartre Marbelle, black Miniature imported and owned by Mrs. Marjorie Tranchin. Photographed in 1977.

# Chapter 16

# *Traveling with Your Dog*

When you travel with your dog, to shows or on vacation or wherever, remember that everyone does not share our enthusiasm or love for dogs and that those who do not, strange creatures though they seem to us, have their rights, too. These rights, on which we should not encroach, include not being disturbed, annoyed, or made uncomfortable by the presence and behavior of other people's pets. Your dog should be kept on lead in public places and should recognize and promptly obey the commands "Down," "Come," "Sit," and "Stay."

Take along his crate if you are going any distance with your dog. And keep him in it when riding in the car. A crated dog has a far better chance of escaping injury than one riding loose in the car should an accident occur or an emergency arise. If you do permit your dog to ride loose, never allow him to hang out a window, ears blowing in the breeze. An injury to his eyes could occur in this manner. He could also become overly excited by something he sees and jump out, or he could lose his balance and fall out.

Never, ever under any circumstances, should a dog be permitted to ride loose in the back of a pick-up truck. I have noted, with horror, that some people do transport dogs in this manner, and I think it cruel and shocking. How easily such a dog can be thrown out of the truck by sudden jolts or an impact! And I am sure that many dogs have jumped out at the sight of something exciting along the way. Some unthinking individuals tie the dog, probably not realizing that were he to jump under those circumstances, his neck would be broken, he could be dragged alongside the vehicle, or he could be hit by another vehicle. If

"Family portrait."
*Left,* Mrs. Edward
Solomon, owner,
with Ch. Gaylasna
Great Expectations.
*Second from left,*
F.C. Dickey with
Gaylasna Whirlwind
and Dassin Stella
Dora. *Next,* Joseph
Vergnetti with Dassin
Diana Diors. *Right,*
June Norjis with
Dassin de la Rose
and Dassin de la
Reese (daughters of
Ch. Dassin Rita La
Rose).

you are for any reason taking your dog in an open back truck, please have sufficient regard for that dog to at least provide a crate for him, and then remember that, in or out of a crate, a dog riding under the direct rays of the sun in hot weather can suffer and have his life endangered by the heat.

If you are staying at a hotel or motel with your dog, exercise him somewhere other than in the flower beds and parking lot of the property. People walking to and from their cars really are not thrilled at "stepping in something" left by your dog. Should an accident occur, pick it up with a tissue or a paper towel and deposit it in a proper receptacle; do not just walk off leaving it to remain there. Usually there are grassy areas on the sides of and behind motels where dogs can be exercised. Use them rather than the more conspicuous, usually carefully tended, front areas or those close to the rooms. If you are becoming a dog show enthusiast, you will eventually need an exercise pen to take with you to the show. Exercise pens are ideal to use when staying at motels, too, as they permit you to limit the dog's roaming space and to pick up after him more easily.

*Left to right:* Most Happy Fella of Camelot, Ch. Wissfire Teddy, and Ch. Camelot's Andrea winning under Mrs. Ramona Van Court. Photo courtesy of Mary Ellen Fishler.

Ch. Roses Fortune of Danique handled by Robert N. Peebles for owner Julie Seabough.

Ch. Sharp's Golden Charm of Kee Woo winning Best Toy Poodle at Santa Barbara Kennel Club in 1970. Owned by Mr. and Mrs. Len Blackwell.

Ch. Valcopy Brando of McKernan, by Ch. Wavir Showboat ex Redfern Camellia. Bred by Dana L. Plonkey and A. McKernan.

Never leave your dog unattended in the room of a motel unless you are absolutely, positively certain that he will stay there quietly and not damage or destroy anything. You do not want a long list of complaints from irate guests, caused by the annoying barking or whining of a lonesome dog in strange surroundings or an overzealous watch dog barking furiously each time a footstep passes the door or he hears a sound from an adjoining room. And you certainly do not want to return to torn curtains or bedspreads, soiled rugs, or other embarrassing evidence of the fact that your dog is not really house-reliable after all.

If yours is a dog accustomed to traveling with you and you are positive that his behavior will be acceptable when left alone, that is fine. But if the slightest uncertainty exists, the wise course is to leave him in the car while you go to dinner or elsewhere; then bring him into the room when you are ready to retire for the night.

When you travel with a dog, it is often simpler to take along from home the food and water he will need rather than buying food and looking for water while you travel. In this way he will have the rations to which he is accustomed and which you know agree with him, and there will be no fear of problems due to different drinking water. Feeding on the road is quite easy now, at least for short trips, with all the splendid dry prepared foods and high-quality canned meats available. A variety of lightweight, refillable water containers can be bought at many types of stores.

If you are going to another country, you will need a health certificate from your veterinarian for each dog you are taking with you, certifying that each has had rabies shots within the required time preceding your visit.

Be careful always to leave sufficient openings to ventilate your car when the dog will be alone in it. Remember that during the summer, the rays of the sun can make an inferno of a closed car within only a few minutes, so leave enough window space open to provide air circulation. Again, if your dog is in a crate, this can be done quite safely. The fact that you have left the car in a shady spot is not always a guarantee that you will find conditions the same when you return. Don't forget that the position of the sun changes in a matter of minutes, and the car you left nicely shaded half an hour ago can be getting full sunlight far more quickly than you may realize. So, if you leave a dog in the car, make sure there is sufficient ventilation and check back frequently to ascertain that all is well.

The lovely and great producing black bitch, Vulcan Wish Upon A Star (Playhouse The Demon King—Vulcan Psychedelic) is now retired to being one of the housepets at Miss A.C. Coppage's Vulcan Kennels. She is the dam of Ch. Vulcan Champagne Starturn, French and Int. Ch. Vulcan Passing Fancy, Ch. Vulcan Champagne Ovature, and Aust. Ch. Vulcan Champagne Ovalord.

# Chapter 17

# Responsibilities of Breeders and Owners

The first responsibility of any person breeding dogs is to do so with care, forethought, and deliberation. It is inexcusable to breed more litters than you need to carry on your show program or to perpetuate your bloodlines. A responsible breeder should not cause a litter to be born without definite plans for the safe and happy disposition of the puppies.

A responsible dog breeder makes absolutely certain, so far as is humanly possible, that the home to which one of his puppies will go is a good home, one that offers proper care and an enthusiastic owner. I have tremendous admiration for those people who insist on visiting (although doing so is not always feasible) the prospective owners of their puppies, to see if they have suitable facilities for keeping a dog, that they understand the responsibility involved, and that all members of the household are in accord regarding the desirability of owning one. All breeders should carefully check out the credentials of prospective purchasers to be sure that the puppy is being placed in responsible hands.

I am certain that no breeder ever wants a puppy or grown dog he has raised to wind up in an animal shelter, in an experimental laboratory, or as a victim of a speeding car. While complete control of such a situation may be impossible, it is at least our responsibility to make every effort to turn over dogs to responsible people. When selling a puppy, it is a good idea to do so with the understanding that should it become necessary to place the dog in other hands, the purchaser will first contact you, the breeder. You may want to help in some way, possibly by buying or taking back the dog or placing it elsewhere. It is not fair just to sell our puppies and then never again give a thought to their welfare. Family problems arise, people may be forced to move where dogs are prohibited, or people just plain grow bored with a dog and its care. Thus the dog becomes a victim. You, as the dog's breeder, should concern yourself with the welfare of each of your dogs and see to it that the dog remains in good hands.

The final obligation every dog owner shares, be there just one dog or an entire kennel involved, is that of making detailed, explicit plans for the future of our dearly loved animals in the event of the owner's death. Far too many of us are apt to procrastinate and leave this very important matter unattended to, feeling that everything will work out or that "someone will see to them." The latter is not too likely, at least not to the benefit of the dogs, unless you have done some advance planning which will assure their future well-being.

Life is filled with the unexpected, and even the youngest, healthiest, most robust of us may be the victim of a fatal accident or sudden illness. The fate of our dogs, so entirely in our hands, should never be left to chance. If you have not already done so, please get together with your lawyer and set up a clause in your will specifying what you want done with each of your dogs, to whom they will be entrusted (after first making absolutely certain that the person selected is willing and able to assume the responsibility), and telling the locations of all registration papers, pedigrees, and kennel records. Just think of the possibilities which might happen otherwise! If there is another family member who shares your love of the dogs, that is good and you have less to worry about. But if your heirs are not dog-oriented, they will hardly know how to proceed or how to cope with the dogs themselves, and they may wind up disposing of or caring for your dogs in a manner that would break your heart were you around to know about it.

In our family, we have specific instructions in each of our wills for each of our dogs. A friend, also a dog person who regards her own dogs with the same concern and esteem as we do ours, has agreed to take over their care until they can be placed accordingly and will make certain that all will work out as we have planned. We have this person's name and phone number prominently displayed in our van and car and in our wallets. Our lawyer is aware of this fact. It is all spelled out in our wills. The friend has a signed check of ours to be used in case of an emergency or accident when we are traveling with the dogs; this check will be used to cover her expense to come and take

Ch. Dhubne Dream Waltz, owned by Carroll Ann Irwin, N. Hollywood, California. Dreamy is the puppy on the cover of *The Book of the Poodle* as a baby with her sire Darth Vader.

over the care of our dogs should anything happen to make it impossible for us to do so. This, we feel, is the least any dog owner should do in preparation for the time our dogs suddenly find themselves without us. There have been so many sad cases of dogs unprovided for by their loving owners, left to heirs who couldn't care less and who disposed of them in any way at all to get rid of them, or left to heirs who kept and neglected them under the misguided idea that they were providing them "a fine home with lots of freedom." All of us *must* prevent any of these misfortunes befalling our own dogs who have meant so much to us!

# Index